ENTERPRISE

RISK

MANAGEMENT

IN

GOVERNMENT:

IMPLEMENTING

ISO 31000:2018

by

James J. Kline Ph.D. CERM

HOW TO ORDER:

Cost is $29.00 per copy plus $6.00 Shipping/Handling in U.S. Offshore orders are based on the form of delivery. Quantity discounts are available from the publisher.

Quality Plus Engineering	503.233.1012|
4052 NE Couch	800.COMPETE
Portland, OR 97232	800.266.7383
USA	GregH@CERMAcademy.com

For bulk purchases, on company letterhead please include information concerning the intended use of the books and the number of books to purchase.

TABLE OF CONTENTS

CHAPTER	**PAGE**
Preface	7
1. A Changing Landscape	15
2. Enterprise Risk Management In Government	47
3. Risk Management Models	59
4. Integrating ERM In the Organization's Culture	77
5. ISO 31000:2018 Overview	101
6. Scope, Context, Criteria	109
7. Risk Identification	123
8. Risk Analysis	141
9. Risk Evaluation	153
10. Risk Treatment	159
11. Recording & Reporting	173
12. Monitoring & Review	183

13. Communication & Consultation   193

14. ERM Performance Evaluation   199

15. Concluding Thoughts   211

PREFACE

This book is a no-frills step-by-step guide for implementing the International Organization for Standardization (ISO) 31000 in government. ISO 31000 is an international standard for implementing Enterprise Risk Management (ERM). It complements other books in the CERM Academy Library. One book, **ISO 31000**, goes into detail on the requirements of ISO 31000. ISO 31000 discusses both public and private sector applications of Enterprise Risk Management.

In addition to the ISO 31000, CERM Academy has a folder entitled 'Governments @ Risk'. This folder includes government Enterprise Risk Management related articles. Some of the material contained in this folder appear in this book. Because of the proliferation of ERM's use at the local government level, the bulk of the examples in this book are from local governments worldwide. This does not mean that other levels of government are not using ERM, far from it. It merely means that in terms of sophistication and application, many local governments are ahead of the pack.

The distribution of government examples is widespread. There are: 1. National, 2. State, 3. Local and 4. Special district examples included. The examples come from Australia, Canada, South Africa, the United Kingdom, and the United States. Twenty-nine additional references are listed after the end notes. These include examples from the departments and agencies of the State of California. Also included are references to two academic studies on ERM implementation and an ERM performance audit.

ISO 31000

As to the emphasis on ISO 31000, it is becoming the dominant standard for governments outside the United States. There are two international risk management standards. One was developed by the Committee of the Sponsoring Organizations of the Treadway Commission (COSO ERM). The other is developed by the International Organization for Standardization. It is designated ISO 31000.

ISO 31000 is the basis for government risk management policies in Australia, Canada, New Zealand and the United Kingdom. It is also the basis of the risk management model mandated by the U.S. Federal Highway Administration (FHWA). The mandate requires all state departments of transportation in the United States to incorporate a Risk Based Asset Management Plan (RBAMP) into their Transportation Asset Management Plan (TAMP) by 2019. The RBAMP format is based on ISO 31000.

ISO 31000 is the dominant Enterprise Risk Management model in government. Understanding ISO 31000 implementation gives the reader knowledge of an administrative process, which is becoming a minimum competency requirement.

The official ISO 31000 standard is about 24 pages long. This book is longer. It presents the key elements of ISO 31000 in their official sequence. For each step, it provides examples drawn from practice. Practical tips and ERM challenges are also presented. The practical tips come from the Victoria State Government Australia 'Practice Guide'. Some of the ERM challenges are drawn from the Chief Financial Officers Council and Performance Improvement Council 'Playbook: Enterprise Risk Management for the U.S. Federal Government'. (Playbook) Others are the author's. The author also makes note of elements in the ISO 31000 sequence which are not well defined or not useful in practice.

Those which are not well defined are discussed in detail. Those which are not useful in practice are mentioned only because ISO has included them in the sequence.

ERM GUIDES

The Victoria Practice Guide and the Playbook are part of a growing body of guides, manuals and frameworks which detail how governments around the world are implementing Enterprise Risk Management. As with OMB and the state of Victoria, most governments develop their own implementation document. Most of these documents are based on ISO 31000.

Generally, the guides list only those elements which the specific organization sees as important. Seldom are examples included in these processes. This book provides substantive examples and discusses their implications for the ERM process.

While the information is presented in the sequence stated in ISO 31000:2018, in practice the steps often occur simultaneously. It should also be noted that while ISO 31000 is the ERM standard designation, it has been revised several times. The most recent being in 2018. Thus, ISO 31000:2018 is the version used as the basis for this book.

It is also used to describe the specific most recent revision, while ISO 31000 references the generic.

MIMIMUM COMPETENCY IN PUBLIC ADMINISTRATION

A few words about the structure of the book. As noted, it is a no frilled presentation of the basics on ISO 31000:2018. However, it is important to understand the environmental circumstances which are increasing the awareness of risk. This is presented in Chapter 1. This chapter stresses the importance of recognizing the multiplicity of the risks facing government and their increasing cost. Continuing to take a siloed approach to risks, seeing them as natural disasters to be handled one way, or Cyber Security to be handled another, is too wasteful of limited resources. Thus, an enterprise wide approach to risk management is necessary.

STRUCTURE OF BOOK

Chapter 2 discusses ERM implementation in government. It also indicates the ways ERM is being pushed by higher levels of government to lower levels. Chapter 3 discusses the two risk models COSO-ERM and ISO 31000:2018. Chapters 4 to 13 discuss the ISO 31000:2018 steps. Chapter 14 discusses the results of two ERM performance audits. One was conducted by the New South Wales Audit Office. The other was conducted by the Audit Office of the Commonwealth of Australia. The audits look at the degree to which ERM has been effectively integrated into their respective organizations. Chapter 15 sums everything up.

Appendix A provides a set of questions developed by Queensland Australia Treasury to help administrators determine the extent of ERM's integration into the organization's culture. It also provides a quick review which can assist management in understanding the ERM implementation process. Appendix B contains questions that the Governing Body and Executive Management can use to make risk mitigation decisions. Appendix C contains the Commonwealth of Australia's ERM mandates. These mandates tell agency and department administrators the specific ERM requirements they need to implement. The mandate also provides a set of standards against which auditors can conduct ERM compliance audits.

Stating that ISO 31000 is the ERM basis for government around the world, does not indicate why any public sector manager should implement ERM. So let's preface several chapters using recent material, not all of which is mentioned in the text.

There are three reasons public sector managers should pay attention. These are:

1. Risk events are increasing in frequency and costs.

2. ERM is increasingly being adopted by federal level governments and pushed to lower level governments.

3. Citizen expect public sector managers to be thrifty in their use of tax dollars.

In Chapter 1 numerous examples are provided of the risks and their costs. A just released report by the European Environmental Agency, adds additional support. Floods, droughts, heatwaves and other extreme weather events have caused European countries €453 billion in damage between 1908 and 2017. "The 33 European Economic Area countries have experienced a collective loss of €33 billion a year since the turn of the decade." (1)

The loss of resources and as will be pointed out in Chapter 1, the human costs, which increase the demand for government services, put strains on resources.

Chapter 2 shows how ERM is being pushed by national and state levels of governments. While the emphasis is on national level efforts, it is important to understand that the impact is global. For instance, the United Nations in its 'Sendai Framework for Disaster Risk Reduction 2015-2030' states:

"It is urgent and critical to anticipate, plan for and reduce disaster risk in order to more effectively protect persons, communities and countries, their livelihoods, health, cultural heritage, socioeconomic assets and ecosystems, and thus strengthen their resilience." (2)

It goes on to state that it is necessary "to use post-disaster recovery and reconstruction to 'Build Back Better'." (3)

This widespread concern and the increasing frequency and costs of risk events, is resulting in a realization that the endless loss and repair cost cycle cannot be sustained. Thus, more emphasis is being placed on prevention and mitigation, to 'Build Back Better'.

While risk assessment and the prevention efforts will occur at the national and state level, more emphasis is going to be placed at the local government level.

In fact, the purpose of ERM is to assist an organization manage all the risks it faces. While the Sendai Framework and organizations like FEMA concentrate of natural disasters, organizations face a wide array of risks. It is this recognition which caused prompted Condoleezza Rice and Amy B. Zegart to write 'Political Risks: How Businesses and Organizations Can Anticipate Global Insecurity.' (4) It is also the reason the World Business Council for Sustainable Development and COSO issued a supplement to COSO-ERM entitled: 'Enterprise Risk Management: Applying Enterprise Risk Management to Environmental, Social And Governance-related Risks'.

Speaking of Environmental Social and Governance (ESG) -related risks the supplement notes:

> "(O)ver the last several decades – and particularly the last 10 years – the prevalence of ESG - related risks has accelerated rapidly. In addition to a clear risk in the number of environmental and social issues that entities now need to consider, the internal oversight, governance and culture for managing these risks also requires greater focus." (5)

It goes on to notes why ERM is increasingly seen as the best way of dealing with these risks.

> "Companies have limited resources, so they cannot respond equally to all risk identified across the entity. For that reason, it is necessary to assess risk for prioritization. Applying ERM to ESG-related risks includes assessing risk severity in a language management can use to prioritize risks." (6)

NEED FOR ERM

The need for ERM is clearly recognized by the World Business Council for Sustainable Development. Since COSO has its own ERM model, it is not surprising that it advocates ERM. However, the need to manage risk is filtering throughout the world. An example comes from an opinion piece by Gary Shapiro, the President and CEO of the Consumer Technology Association.

In his piece, he notes that his awareness for the need to manage risk is the result of three event: Hurricane Maria, which devasted Puerto Rico, the killing of 58 people in the Las Vega outdoor concert, and the wildfires in California. Because of these events he began to think about resilience and recognized the "need to avoid, withstand and recover from such tragedies." He states:

> "Thinking ahead helps make the unexpected expected, It's not just about peace of mind. It's about knowing that, in the face of tragedy, preparedness and resilience can keep or cities, communities and homes safe, powered, warm and secure." (7)

This statement sums up the expectation the public has with respect to managing risks. It also makes it clear why the adoption of ERM is critical. It is to help make our "cities and communities and homes safe, powered, warm and secure."

This expectation is global. Public administrators can no longer view risks as isolated and siloed. To effectively deal with them, within the confines of limited resources, a proactive enterprise wide approach is required.

In short, for those individuals charged with managing public monies and resources, and those deciding to accept this responsibility, ERM is fast becoming a minimum competency. This book helps current and future public sector managers obtain this level of competency.

If you would like to share your thoughts, please reach out to me at: Jeffreyk12011@live.com

CHAPTER 1:
CHANGING PUBLIC LANDSCAPE

INTRODUCTION

This chapter discusses the variety of risks that governmental organizations face. It also shows that because of their increasing costs, there is a growing need to mitigate the damage caused by risk events.

TIMES THEY ARE A'CHANGING

President Trump recently tweeted "Billions of dollars are sent to the State of California for forest fires that, with proper Forest Management, would never happen. Unless they get their act together, which is unlikely, I have ordered FEMA (Federal Emergency Management Agency) to send no more money. It is a disgraceful situation in lives & money!"

GOVERNMENT RESPONSE

This tweet reflects the growing concern that the way governments have responded to natural disasters and other risks need to change. It also indicates that the federal government can no longer be counted on to provide all the money needed to recover from the damages due to natural disasters or other significant risk events. (A risk event is an occurrence that usually has an adverse impact on the organization and the accomplishment of its mission. The adverse impact can be a monetary cost, the inability to achieve a specified objective or strategic goal or have a negative impact on the organization's reputation.)

The U.S. federal government is not the only government which is facing this issue and considering different approaches. The Organization for Economic Cooperation and Development (OECD) in its policy guide for boosting resilience states:

> "The scale of recent impacts has raised questions about whether OECD member countries could have made more progress in their risk management systems to increase resilience against such shocks through better risk prevention and mitigation." (1)

This concern is particularly troubling when one considers that too often there is a lack of insurance to cover damage caused by natural disasters. The Actuaries Institute and Australian Local Government Association are pressing for an increase in mitigation spending in federal budget submissions. It is estimated that only 40% of Australia's annual natural peril costs of $11-12 billion are insured. The proposal is for the federal government and states to co-contribute $200 million a year to a mitigation fund and that local governments be required to budget for natural disaster costs. (2)

Aon, a global re-insurance broker estimates the 394 natural disasters in 2018 cost the re-insurance industry $90 billion or 40% of the total $225 billion in economic loses. Further, 2017 and 2018 were the costliest back-to-back years for both economic losses ($653 billion) and insured losses across all hazards ($237 billion). (3)

> "Among the takeaways from the events of 2018 was the recognition that catastrophic risk continues to evolve. The complex combination of socioeconomics, shifts in population and exposure into vulnerable locations, plus a changing

climate contribution to more volatile weather patterns, is forcIng new conversations to sufficiently handle the need for mitigation and resilience measures." (4)

This paragraph sums up nicely what has been called the VUCA environment. VUCA stands for Volatility, Uncertainty, Complexity and Ambiguity. This term has been used by governments, the private sector and the military to describe the dynamic risk laden 21st century environment most organizations find themselves operating in.

This complex combination means that a natural disaster in one part of the world, can cascade throughout the globally connected economic system. It also means that the destructive nature of some of these risks and their frequency create an environment which is both uncertain and volatile.

The following examples demonstrate the complexity and difficulty governments face with respect to the risk laden global environment.

EXAMPLES OF NATURAL DISASTERS

FLOODING IN THAILAND
In 2011, Thailand experienced massive flooding. The United Nations estimated that this flood reduced global industrial production by 2.5% and that the top three non-life insurance companies paid out $5.3 billion in claims. This creates uncertainty locally because the exact impact is not immediately known, nor can it be easily, because the event is worlds away, remedied by local government action.(5)

Even when the event is localized, the complex impact of a natural disasters makes it difficult for governments to respond. An example is the cyclone in 2014 in the Visakhapatnam District in India.

VISAKHAPATNAM DISTRICT IN INDIA

In 2014, the Visakhapatnam District in India was hit by a cyclone with winds up to 250 miles per hour. It caused an estimated $3.4 billion in damages. As a result of the cyclone, communication was crippled, and disaster response delayed. Mobile networks were disrupted. Transportation was hindered by downed trees and flooded highways. Power was out for 3 days in the city and up to a month in some rural areas. While the water system was not damaged, without power no fresh water could be pumped. (6)

The cyclone caused widespread damage and required responses to multiple areas from repairing transportation network for disaster relief, to getting communication systems up and running so repairs and relief can be coordinated, to getting electricity back so fresh water can be distributed. Such a circumstance puts government officials in an ambiguous position. What action takes priority, given limited resources? At the same time, the public, higher levels of government and victims are demanding immediate response and relief.

An even more complex problem arises when the government is all but wiped out.

PARADISE CALIFORNIA CAMP FIRE

The town of Paradise California, U.S. was effectively wiped out by the 2018 California Camp Fire. It had an insurance claim for $64 million. However, its insurance company had only $23 million in reserve. The Paradise and other claims forced the company into bankruptcy. As a result of this bankruptcy, the unpaid claims will either not be paid or will have to be covered by the state of California. (7)

The question for government officials of Paradise is how to rebuild. The more unpaid claims the state must pick up, the more pressure is added to the state budget. This can lead to delays in the receipt of the resources needed to rebuild. Yet, some basic municipal operation needs to occur, if the city is to rebuild.

Even when the natural disaster leaves the government operation viable, there are costs which impact more than the infrastructure.

COSTS OF NATURAL DISASTERS

OREGON (U.S.) EAGLE CREEK WILDFIRE

In 2017, the Oregon Eagle Creek Wildfire burned 48,831 acers of forest land. One hundred and seventy-six hikers had to be rescued. Over one thousand people had to be evacuated. Businesses in the Cascades Locks area lost between $2 - $3 million. For ten days the westbound Instate 84, the main east west interstate, was closed. For three days no trains could use the Union Pacific Railroad track near the fire area. River traffic on the Columbia River was closed. The cost for fighting the fire was $20 million. Thus, the fire had an impact beyond the immediate fire damaged area. (8)

OTTAWA CANADA TORNADO

On September 2018 a Category 2 tornado hit the west end of Ottawa Canada. The tornado damaged Hydro One's Merivale transmission stations and power lines. The cost to the company is estimated to be $10 million. Two earlier tornados cost the company $2.6 million. The $10 million cost exceeded the company's $3.1 million contingency for emergency repairs. The City of Ottawa experienced damage to three community centers and one of the city's garages. The cost of repair is estimated to be $750,000. The $750,000 is just below the minimum eligible for federal reimbursement. (9) The repair costs must be borne by existing revenue. The shifting of funds to cover repair costs means that funds are not going to be available for other priorities.

CALIFORNIA WILDFIRES

It is estimated that the 2018 wildfires in California will cost the state's economy $400 billion. This is in addition to fighting increasingly costly wildfires. The California Department of Forestry and Fire Protection's request for firefighting money from the state emergency fund has increased from $90 million in 2010 to $947 million in 2017. This continual drain on California's reserves reduces the ability of the state to make itself more resilient. (10)

NATIONAL OCEANOGRAPHIC AND ATMOSPHERIC DAMAGE ASSESSMENT

A National Oceanographic and Atmospheric Administration report on the impact of weather and climate disasters indicates that in 2018 natural disasters cost the state of North Carolina between 3-5% of its Gross State Product. The damage in Florida and Georgia was the equivalent of 2-3% of these state's gross domestic product.(11) The more that states are required to spend on recovering from natural disasters, the less is available for normal operations, let alone to fund major systems and infrastructure upgrades.

U.S. GOVERNMENT FIRE SUPPRESSION COST

At the U.S. federal level, the cost for fire suppression has increased 562% over the last twenty years. Here again, the pressure on budgets is significant. Competition for funds is increasing.

A national study estimates that it will cost between $45-70 billion a year for at least 20 years to improve the country's infrastructure. This cost includes rebuilding pavement, bridges, and other highway assets. The investment in basic infrastructure repair is needed before they become unserviceable. This does not include the upgrades needed for ensuring the highway systems are capable of handling self-driving vehicles and smart highways technology. (12)

With the demand on federal resources for disaster relief continuing to rise, and projections that climate change will cause superstorms and increase natural disasters, combined with the normal operating demands and that of repairing and upgrading existing systems, federal officials are floating ideas to redistribute more of the recovery burden to state and local governments.

In an April 2019 report entitled 'Expected Cots of Damage From Hurricane winds and Storm-Related Flooding', the Congressional Budget Office listed "increasing the share of disaster assistance paid for by state and local governments", as one of the policy option Congress should consider. (13)

The federal government is not the only organization finding that the costs of natural disasters are increasing. Local governments are also seeing their cost rise.

CALGARY – INCREASING INSURABLE LOSSES

An early snow in 2014 resulted in $34 million in non-insurable losses. In 2013, a flood impacted over 89,000 in 32 communities. The flood required the evacuation of 6,000 homes and 4,000 businesses. There was over $400 million in damages to municipal infrastructure. The Bonnybrook wastewater treatment plant was flooded. Light rail transit tunnels were flooded. Sixteen Light rail transit stations were closed, as were 22 bridges and numerous roads. Municipal, provincial and federal government complexes, Calgary Zoo, Stampede grounds and Saddledome, recreation facilities and schools closed.

After the flood, in order to get re-insured, the city was forced to go to multiple insurance providers. Initially insurance premiums increased 100%. The premiums were later reduced to pre-flood levels after the city-initiated resilience actions.

Since the 2013 flood, the city has committed $150 million to various flood mitigation and resilience projects. As of 2018, 11 projects have been completed, with another 16 in progress. It is estimated that the completed projects have mitigated flood damage by 30%, compared to 2013. (14)

SOCIAL IMPACTS OF DISASTERS

While economic losses are understood and tracked, as are the costs associated with the rebuilding and repairing of roads, bridges, and utilities, other impacts are seldom tracked. For instance, homeowners who are not covered by insurance go bankrupt. Aon estimates that of the 2018 claims from natural disasters in the United States, only $90 billion (40%) of the $225 billon were covered by insurance companies. The United Nations Refugee Agency estimates that between 30 to 60 percent of the disaster survivors experience post-traumatic stress disorder. (15)

QUEENSLAND AUSTRALIA FLOOD

The human and social service costs are often greater than the physical repair costs. For instance, a study of the cost of the floods in Queensland Australia from 2011-12 found that the increase in diabetes and cardiovascular disease and the development of strokes cost $430 million Australian dollars. The family violence resulting from the stress cost about $720 million. Infrastructure repair costs were $450 million. (16)

Natural disasters then, can create both short- and long-term drains on government resources. The short-term costs are associated with dealing with and repairing the damage caused by the natural disaster. The long-term cost are the social and economic costs which linger long after the repairs to infrastructure are made.

INCREASING PUBLIC RISKS

Unfortunately, natural disasters are not the only risks which can adversely impact government resources. In fact, because natural disasters are not spread equally it is too easy for government administrators to ignore the potential impact of both natural disasters and other risk events.

Below are some examples of risk events that have impacted governments around the world.

LLOYD'S OF LONDON RISK ASSESSMENT - *RISK EVENT*
A Lloyd's of London report entitled 'Cities at Risk' identified twenty-two threats to the 279 largest cities in the world. These include market crashes, human pandemics, floods, civil conflicts, cyber-attacks, social unrest, plant epidemics, power outages and nuclear accidents. The total cost of the risks is estimated to be $546.5 billion. (17)

U.S. DEPARTMENT OF VETERANS AFFAIRS MEDICAL CARE SYSTEM FAILURE - *DAMAGE TO REPUTATION*
In 2014, it was reported in the press that veterans seeking care from the U.S. Veterans Health Administration were not receiving the care promised. In fact, some were dying, because they could not get scheduled for medical care.

An internal investigation, by the Veterans Administration, found that 120,000 veterans were left waiting for or never received care. Moreover, thirty-five veterans had died while awaiting care. The investigation also determined that managers falsified records to make it look like the veterans were receiving timely care. Obama's Deputy Chief of Staff described the environment at the Veterans Administration as "significant and chronic system failure" and a "corrosive culture". (18)

FLINT MICHIGAN WATER CONTAMINATION – *HEALTH HAZARD*

On July 30, 2016, six more Michigan (U.S.) state employees were charged with misconduct in Flint Michigan Water crisis. The state alleges that employees of the environmental quality agency failed to ensure that corrosion-control was added to the water supply. This failure caused lead to leak into the water supply. The contamination resulted in thousands of children in Flint Michigan being exposed to toxins. Further, some residents had to drink bottled water for more than two years. (19)

NEW YORK CITY – FRAUD BY CONTRACTOR

On April 30, 2014 three individuals were sentenced for defrauding New York City of over $100 million in a "botched automated payroll project". The automated payroll project cost ballooned from $63 million to over $700 million. In the process the contractor allegedly accepted kickbacks, funneled money to shell companies, deposited the stolen money into overseas bank accounts, inflated bills and charged for inflated payrolls, some of whom were fired employees.

The three each received 20-year prison terms for their part in the fraud. The fraud tarnished New York City Mayor Bloomberg's reputation, since he had promised to bring a business ethos and latest technology to New York City. During Mayor Bloomberg's twelve years in office, he increased the portion of the city's contracting budget by about a third, to more than $10 billion. (20)

CITY OF ATLANTA GEORGIA – RANSOMWARE CYBER-ATTACK

On March 22, 2018, the City of Atlanta (U.S) was the victim of a ransomware cyber-attack. Because of the attack, there were computer outages to numerous city department. Residences attempting to pay bills or access court information could not do so, because computer systems were down. The Mayor advised city employees and residents to contact their credit agencies and monitor their bank accounts. The Federal Bureau of Investigation and the Department of Homeland Security also assisted with the investigation. The city spent $9 million to correct the problem. (21)

MACOMB COUNTY SEWAGE LEAK - *HUMAN ERROR*
A human error weakened an underground sewer line. It collapsed creating a mass sink hole. The result was a 'tsunami of sewage'. It cost $70 million to repair the line. (22)

NEW ORLEANS - PREVENTIVE MAINTENANCE ISSUES
Several weeks before Hurricane Harvey hit Louisiana, the City of New Orleans was struggling to get fifteen water pumps online. The lack of working pumps had caused serious flooding throughout the city several weeks earlier. In one instance, a man in a wheelchair had to be rescued from a flooded street. The flood waters were pushing his wheelchair down the street. He told his rescuers he was in fear for his life. In other instance, the rushing water caught people trying to get home, pushing their cars off the road or down the street. The experience brought back memories of Katrina and associated mental trauma. (23)

OREGON PUBLIC EMPLOYEE RETIREMENT SYSTEM – *LEGACY SYSTEM*
The Oregon Public Employee Retirement System (PERS) is the retirement program for all state and local government employees in Oregon. Like many such retirement systems in the United States, it has a substantial unfunded liability. As of 2018, the unfunded liability amounts to $26.6 billion. In 2013, the state legislature tried to amend some of the provisions that got PERS into financial trouble. However, the Oregon Supreme Court threw out most of the money saving provisions. Since that time, the unfunded liability has grown.

Generally, the PERS investment fund has returned around 6.03% over the last ten years. This can be compared to the 7.5% expected rate. The deficit means that the state, schools and local governments must make up the difference. The estimated increase in pension contribution is $2.1 billion statewide for the 2021-23 biennium. That is a 45% increase over the 2018-20 biennium costs. This continuing increase in pension contributions takes money away from other organizational activities. (24)

COMPETITION FOR PUBLIC RESOURCES

It far too easy to look only at the most immediate risk. Such an approach means that when resources are diverted to cover the immediate costs required for repair and recovery, other needs are left unfunded. Infrastructure is one example.

INFRASTRUCTURE
The American Society of Civil Engineers (ASCE) estimates that it will require at least $65 billion to repair California's dams, waterways, roads and bridges. In fact, the ASCE gave California the moron prize as the worst state in the nation because of its infrastructure issues. (25) California is not the only state facing similar problems. It is estimated that the state of Georgia will need to spend $12 billion on sewage, water and infrastructure improvements. (26)

A 2016 Canadian Infrastructure Report Card indicates that almost 60% of its infrastructure is owned by local government. The value of the municipal infrastructure is $1.1 trillion (Canadian). Thirty-five percent of this infrastructure needs attention. At the current rate of local government investment, additional infrastructure will need attention. "Investing in preventive maintenance and regular repair will prolong the asset service life, avoiding premature and costly reconstruction and service disruption."(27) But in order to manage this cost long range planning will be needed, which includes use of new technology and better ways of dealing with the impact of extreme weather events.

LIMITED RESOURCES
As the examples above show, events which adversely impact government resources - staff time, money - or its reputation, can come from many quarters. The natural disaster repair estimates, infrastructure repair and social costs indicate, going forward the budgets of governments at all levels are going to be stressed. Consequently, governments at all levels are recognizing that with limited resources and increasing demands, the costs of risks events need to be managed. Further, this must be done in a systematic and proactive manner. It can no longer be limited to a few chosen areas such as natural disasters or cyber-attacks. A dollar spent, when all or part of that expenditure could have been avoided, is a dollar wasted.

NEED TO MANAGE PUBLIC RISKS USING RISK MANAGEMENT

It is becoming obvious that a comprehensive approach to risk management is needed to deal with the issue of multiple risks and increasing costs. This comprehensive approach is called Enterprise Risk Management (ERM). This recognition can be seen in the statements of various governments around the world.

MCKAY COUNCIL AUSTRALIA
The McKay Council of Australia notes:

"As a public authority it is exposed to a broad range of risks which, if not managed, could adversely impact on the organisation achieving its strategic objectives." (28)

DENBIGHSHIRE UNITED KINGDOM

Denbighshire in the United Kingdom, in its Guide to Risk Management echoes the above.

"We recognize that there are risks involved in all our activities and that we have a duty to manage these risks in a balanced, structured and cost-effective way. Therefore, the process for identifying, assessing, controlling and monitoring risk is considered an integral part of our management process. As a result, we are able to enhance service delivery capabilities and better achieve our priorities and value for money." (29)

UNITED STATES FEDERAL GOVERNMENT

The U.S. Government Accountability Office, (GAO) in its '2018 High Risk Report' to the U.S. Congress states: "The consistent and regular use of ERM can help agency leaders identify and mange risks, including high-risk issues."(30)

The Chief Financial Officers Council and Performance Improvement Council in 'Playbook: Enterprise Risk Management (ERM) for the U.S. Federal Government' go even further:

"Risk is unavoidable in carrying out an organization's objectives. Government departments and agencies exist to deliver services that are in the public interest, especially in areas where the private sector is either unable or unwilling to do so. This work is surrounded by uncertainty, which both poses threats to success and offers opportunity for increasing value to the American people.

While agencies cannot respond to all risks, one of the most salient lessons from past crises and negative reputational incidents is that both public and private sector organizations would benefit from establishing or reviewing and strengthening their risk management practices. Agencies are well advised to work to the greatest extent possible to identify, evaluate, and manage challenges related to mission delivery and manage risk to a tolerable level." (31)

ADMINISTRATIVE BENEFITS
Yuma County Arizona
In 2018, Yuma County's 'Enterprise Risk Management: Addressing Uncertainty, Improving Decision-Making', was an Achievement Award Winner. The award was issued by the National Association of Counties. Yuma County indicates that their ERM program has been effective in helping manage uncertainty and improved strategic decision making. It has also resulted in cost savings and improved organizational communication. (32)

Recognizing the need to manage risks is one thing. To be effective and valuable, ERM must demonstrate the positive impact noted by Yuma County. The positive impact can be expressed in several ways. The two most common are improved administrative efficiency and cost reductions.

WORCESTER SHIRE COUNCIL
The Worcester Shire Council of the United Kingdom lists the administrative benefits of ERM. These are:

- Informing strategic/operational decision-making.

- Safeguarding all persons to whom the Council has a duty of care, including employees.

- Increasing chances of success and reducing chances of failure.

- Enhancing stakeholder value by minimising losses and max-imising opportunities.

- Increasing knowledge and understanding of exposure to risk.

- Enabling not just backward-looking review, but forward-look-ing thinking.

- Contributing towards Corporate Social Responsibility and sus-tainable development.

- Reducing unexpected and costly surprises.

- Minimising vulnerability to fraud and corruption.

- Providing management with early warnings of problems.

- Ensuring minimal service disruption.

- Ensuring statutory compliance.

- Better targeting of resources i.e. focusses scarce resources on high risk activity.

- Reducing the financial costs (e.g. due to service disruption, lit-igation, insurance premiums and claims, and bad investment decisions).

- Delivering creative and innovative projects. and

- Protecting the Shire's reputation. (33)

The Worcester Shire list is like those reported by other governments around the world. The combined impact of any three or four of these benefits should provide justification for implementing ERM. ERM pro-vides better targeting of resources, reduces financial costs, provides public management warning of possible problems and reduces costly surprises.

This list indicates ERM provides substantive administrative benefits. It also contributes to value protection.

EFFICIENCY AND REVENUE ENHANCEMENT

In Commonwealth countries like Australia, Canada, New Zealand and the United Kingdom a common term used is value for money. In the United States this term translates to efficiency.

ELECTRIC POWER BOARD OF CHATTANOOGA

The Electric Power Board (EPB) of Chattanooga Tennessee is an example of how a risk mitigation effort can result in efficiency improvements and revenue enhancement.

Volkswagen wanted to build a plant in the Chattanooga area, but was concerned with the frequency of tornado caused power outages. To help ensure the development of the plant, EPB agreed to upgrade its system to fiber optics and include automated switching, which would reduce the chances of power outages.

In the process of upgrading, EPB installed automated meter reading and added high speed Internet. The automated meter reading resulted in an annual saving of $1.6 million. Automated switching for one storm in 2012 saved EPB over $1 million in overtime costs. In addition, High Speed Internet added substantively to EPB's revenue stream. Thus, in the process of mitigating the risk of tornado caused power outages, EPB enhanced its efficiency and revenue stream.

There were also spillover effects from the offering of high-speed Internet. In order to offer it, EPB had to succeed in state court against the cable company and before the Federal Communication Commission. Because it was successful, it received positive press. In addition, the availability of high-speed Internet, allowed the city to develop incubators sites where businesses, which needed high-speed Internet, could grow and thrive. The result was increased economic development activity. The city was designated a 'Gig City'. This designation enhanced its reputation. (34)

COST SAVINGS

ERM can also help reduce the cost of adverse risk impact.   While the Lloyd's study does not identify specific mitigative actions, it notes that an increase in local government resilience (mitigative actions), would reduce the adverse impact by $73.4 billion or 13.4%. Such reductions conserves resources. (35)

NATIONAL INSTITUTE OF BUILDING SCIENCE STUDY

A 2017 study by the National Institute of Building Science is more specific. For every dollar spent towards obtaining and utilizing Housing and Community Development Block Grants, Economic Development Administration grants and Federal Emergency Management Agency (FEMA) Flood Mitigation Assistance and Hazard Mitigation grants, to improve resilience, six dollars in future damages were saved. This includes the reduction in future deaths and Post Traumatic Stress, repair costs for damaged buildings, lost revenue to households, loss of economic activity to the broader community, the loss of public services such as fire stations, hospital and other public buildings because of the damage caused by the natural hazard and the cost of search and rescue. In addition, for every dollar added to the costs associated with ensuring building codes exceed the 2015 International Building Code and the International Residential Code, four dollars in future damage is saved. (36)

Mitigative efforts reduce the adverse impact of risk events. The two studies above and the experience of Calgary demonstrate this point.

ERM can help an organization develop and achieve their strategic objectives. Two common strategic objectives of governments worldwide are to make the organization more resilient and to become a digital government/smart city.

RESILIENCE

Resilience is a much-discussed topic in the public sector. With the increased frequency of natural disasters and their repair costs, how to improve resilience and reduce these costs has become necessary.

WHY GOVERNMENTS MUST BE RESILIENT

Canada's National Round Table on the Environment and the Economy lists three reason government must act to become more resilient. These are:

1. Doing nothing would expose an organization's assets, services, customers and employees to the full impact of extreme weather events and climate change impacts such as increasing Green House Gas emissions and rising energy cost. Doing nothing also impedes the ability to meet organizational objectives and the expectations of investors, customer, employees and taxpayers.

2. Citizens who depend on municipal services expect decision-makers to take climate change into account when planning, building and operating infrastructure to maintain series into the future.

3. While significant risks will arise from climate change, risk mitigation measures can create new opportunities for growth and prosperity, such as drought resistant tree breeds and innovative engineering solutions. Communities expect

opportunities for growth and prospects to be realized. (37)

STAGES OF RESILIENCE

The National Academies of Sciences states: "Resilience is the ability to prepare and plan for, absorb, recover from and more successfully adapt to adverse events."(38)   Under this definition there are four stages:

- Stage 1 is to prepare and plan for the risk.

- Stage 2 is to absorb the consequences of the risk.

- Stage 3 is to recover from the risk event.

- Stage 4 is to successfully adapt to the risk event.

The ability to successfully manage these steps helps determine the resilience of the organization. Resilience ultimately means the organization uses a standardized, proactive approach to risk management. Enterprise Risk Management is an example of such a holistic standardized approach.

Stage 1 is directly related to ERM. The steps in the ERM process help the organization to, in a systematic manner, identify the risks it faces, prioritize those risks and determine mitigative actions.   In other words, ERM is step one. ERM can also assist with the negotiation of the other three stages. By understanding the degree to which the mitigative actions are effective, management understands where problems can arise. This helps with response planning and recovery. In addition, ERM requires continual planning and assessment

Improved resilience is a current objective of federal, state and local governments. Another strategic objective is to become a digital government and smart cities.

DIGITAL GOVERNMENT/SMART CITIES

Digital Government and Smart City development is the technological extension of Electronic (E) Government. E Government is government's use of computer and electronic devices. There are two objectives for E Government. The first is to improve communication with citizens. The second is to improve operational efficiency.

With the improvement of microprocessors and the expansion of the Internet, everyday devices and government facilities are increasingly being linked. For cities, this linkage includes traffic signals, trash receptacles, and water and wastewater systems among others. By linking them and having the devices communicate means they are providing information. Government can use this information to improve operational efficiency and customer service. The interconnection of such devices via the Internet is termed 'Internet of Things' (IoT). The linkage of government activities and process through the Internet is termed digital government and smart cities.

HOMELAND SECURITY REPORT

A U.S. Center for Infrastructure Protection and Homeland Security (CIP) report lists the following as the general practices being incorporated into smart cities. These are:

1. **Smart Governance and Education** – Extension of governments uses of technology to communicate with citizens and the use of on-line interactive educational courses.

2. **Smart Healthcare** – Digitization of patient information, remote monitoring and other applications, such as surgery and consultation, to provide better patient care.

3. **Smart Building** – Lighting, heating and security linked via the

Internet and accessible via mobile devices or computers.

4. **Smart Mobility** – Driverless vehicles, sensors on roadways, traffic monitoring and warnings provided to mobile devices.

5. **Smart Infrastructure** – Embedding of sensors into the infrastructure to provide information on traffic congestion and traffic counts.

6. **Smart Technology** – Use of technology to collect and communicate information and control devices, such as automatic switching on power grids and automatic meter reading.

7. **Smart Energy** – Thermostats which monitor room temperature can be adjusted remotely to save energy, solar panels which automatically adjust to the movement of sun, and automatic adjustment of lighting based on the movement of building occupants.

8. **Smart Citizens** – Governments' use of crowd sourcing information to develop information on crime, environmental problems, traffic accidents etc. on a real time basis. (39)

The development of this interconnect network creates risk. While the risks to physical technology and infrastructure are known, as are the risks associated with cyber-attacks, the risks associated with integrating the three are not fully understood but are obvious.

The interconnectivity and expansion of IoT gives attackers multiple ways to attack a public infrastructure system. It also creates other risks such as:

- Loss of visibility into all the parts of the system mean problems may not be immediately recognized.

- Cascading failures can occur, since humans will not be presence in areas of the system they once were. They, therefore, might not be able to prevent the cascading effect.

- Unanticipated permutations of automated functions. The complexity of the integrated systems might create unanticipated and unintended problems.

- Unintentional elimination of manual overrides. Without as many humans present and the number of manual overrides reduced, the likelihood of the adverse impact of a cascading failure is increased. (40)

CHALLENGES

The expansion of smart city funding and the desire to become a digital government or smart city, is creating several other challenges. Chief among them are economic, technical and risk management. The economic challenge arises because of the replacement and repair costs associated with new technologies. Incorporating IoT into existing infrastructure can be costly. The cost may be greater than citizens may want to authorize. Technological and risk management challenges arise because of the lack of security associated with IoT.

Some smart cities have already experienced malicious attacks, unintentional collapses of critical infrastructure and systemic failure that quickly spread through the systems networks. In many cases, network security problems arise because the older technology is not totally compatible with the new technology. This can create security gaps which, as noted above, can be exploited by attackers.

The risk management problem is particularly acute because the city becomes focused on problems associated with the immediate project and forgets to take a holistic view, or to make the necessary investment in cyber-security. (41)

SMART CITY GROWTH

In 2016, there were approximately 1.6 billion IoT devices in the United States. By 2020 it is estimated that there will be more than 30 billion such devices. It is estimated that local governments will invest $41 trillion over the next twenty years in smart city development.(42) In addition, in 2017 the Department of Transportation (DoT) allocated $165 million for smart city development.(43) The DoT funding is focused on the development of solutions to ease congestion and improve pedestrian and driver safety. The National Science Foundation allocated $60 million to smart city development. The money is for tracking air quality, noise, and traffic congestion.

The commitment of both federal and local governments in the United States is reflected by similar commitments by other governments and municipal governments. Canada and India have initiated national smart city grants. In addition, cities such as Singapore, Dubai, Barcelona and Amsterdam are already considered smart cities.

As noted above, a major problem is the outdated nature of some governmental software as the following indicates:

> "For local officials throughout the country, the shift from old-school servers to rented cloud storage has made it tougher than ever to fund upgrades. They can budget physical equipment as capital expenses, meaning they could issue bonds to pay for them. But cloud computing is a service, ... which means officials have to pay for it with operating funds - the same pool of money that goes toward addressing more tangible demands, such as parks and cops." (44)

This competition for funds often leads to neglect. The following examples show the problems associated with this competition for funds.

COST TO UPGRAGE LEGACY NETWORKS SYSTEMS

Below are some examples of legacy computer and network systems and the cost associated with upgrading them. (45)

BALTIMORE – POLICE DEPARTMENT
The system for storing and tracking crime reports is more than 20 years old, doesn't comply with the national incident reporting system, and can't link to other data bases. This situation adversely affects national security and crime fighting. Cost to upgrade: $4 million

BROOME COUNTY NEW YORK – OFFICE OF EMERGENCY SERVICES
The County has twelve different radio-systems with portions dating to the 1970's. This prevents communications among systems. Lack of communication among systems can hinder emergency response and endanger lives in the event of an emergency. Cost of upgrade: $23 million.

PHILADELPHIA – STREETS DEPARTMENT
The control systems for most of the city's 3,000 traffic signals date to the 1960's. This makes it harder for the department to manage congestion. Cost to upgrade: $175,000 to $735,000 per intersection.

MINNESOTA – VEHICLE LICENSING SOFTWARE
The state of Minnesota spent $100 million over a ten-year period to replace its vehicle-licensing and registration software. Once installed there were so many glitches that another $16 million was requested

to fix the problems.

As noted earlier, the risks associated with patching legacy systems and linking legacy to newer systems, creates opportunities for hackers to disrupt the system. Such disruption can result in loss of life. However, the cost of updating the systems is substantive and often faces opposition from the public, because of cost overruns like that experience by the state of Minnesota.

SMART CIY APPLICATION NEED NOT TO BE EXPENSIVE
ERM can help management identify and prioritize the risks it faces. It helps it focus mitigative actions which can be incorporated into the organization's strategic plan. This provides a degree of assurance that resources are going to be allocated in an efficient and effective manner.

Such risk analysis and risk-based thinking can also help avoid bad press and enable the organization to reduce the adverse impact of the risks. Further, such action does not necessarily have to result in large capital projects. It can result in the taking of mitigative actions which are smaller in scope. Non-revenue Water Loss and the Virginia Beach StormSense provide two such examples.

NON-REVENUE WATER LOSS
Smart cities applications cannot meet all the infrastructure-related needs in the energy and water sectors. However, they can help cities and counties make efficient use of limited resources.

Real-time monitoring can detect problems in the systems, such as equipment failures, leaks, or contaminants before the damage is too great.

Currently, an estimated $2.6 billion is lost every year as water mains leak treated drinking water. Non-revenue water (NRW) results in the waste of an important resource, particularly in water-scarce regions, and prevents utilities from realizing revenue that can be reinvested in their systems. (46)

The city of Boulder Colorado is an example of a city which is tackling NRW. Boulder has compiled a database of water pipes throughout the city. The database includes information on the date of water pipe installation, age, history of breakage, and material. These data can be used to predict which pipes are most likely to fail so that they can be replaced before they do, reducing the public impact. (46)

In the case of Non-Revenue Water Loss, the work can be done by existing staff, since it requires compilation and analysis of existing data. Once analysed, a pipe replacement schedule can be developed and incorporated into future capital improvement projects. The reduction of leakage protects water resources and enhances revenue at the same time.

The following case study provides another example of small project risk mitigation.

Virginia Beach Stormsense – Case Study
The City of Virginia Beach provides a case study for the combined use of the IoT to improve resilience and mitigate flood damage by providing flooding notification to residents 36 hours ahead of time. Partnering with the Virginia Institute of Marine Science (VIMS), the city created StromSense. StromSense is a program which involves the installation of multiple sensors in the Hampton Road area to monitor water levels. (Hampton Road along the Virginia coast is considered the second most densely populated area in the United States at risk from

rising sea levels. New Orleans being number one.) The sensors com-
plement existing sensors which gauge water levels, stream flows and
rainfall. The new sensors are designed to improve real-time data on
street level flooding.

The sensor Information allows for customer-tailored assessment of
neighborhood flooding risks and the development of effective mitigation efforts.

In 2015, the Public Works Department funded ten water levels sensors
with weather stations to measure water level, air pressure, wind
speed and rainfall. The sensors cost $38,000 each. In 2016 the city
joined eight other cities in the Hampton Roads region to participate in
NIST's Global City Teams Challenge. The consortium won a $75,000
prize in the 'Replicable Smart City Technology' category. StormSense
has been awarded funding and prize money amounting to $500,000.
City staff estimates that the early warning has reduced the costs of
flooding. (47)

While the Non-Revenue Water Loss and Smart Sense examples show
how small smart city projects can have substantive payoff, the lack of
funding, outdated software and the complexity of the Internet of
Things, also indicate that if smart cities and digital government is to
become a reality, a different approach to assessing how resources are
to be allocate and managed, needs to occur.

ERM AND SMART CITY PROJECTS

One such approach was used by the Indian National government. It
required, as part of its smart city grant application, that risks be identified along with mitigative actions to be taken. Such action indicates

that the government is attempting to address ahead of time the problems which can cause cost overruns and project delays.

CITY OF VADODARA SMART CITY MITIGATION

Below is part of the risk section from the Smart City Challenge Stage 2 application from the Indian City of Vadodara.(48) It shows the projects risks, their likely impact and the mitigative action to be taken.

While the risks and mitigative actions are specific to the Smart City Project, the fact that the application requires risk identification, is indicative of two things. First, project such as this are complex, and it is better to start thinking about the risks and mitigative efforts early. Second, in the case of India, the national government expects mitigative efforts to be in place and carried out during implementation.

SUMMARY

The number of natural disasters is increasing in intensity, frequency and cost. It is becoming apparent a cycle of unending and ever-increasing expenditure is beginning. This realization has caused President Trump to raise concerns about California's lack of wildfire mitigation efforts. The continuing drain of resources for infrastructure repair and other risks such as cyber-attacks is causing a rethink on how risk mitigation should be handled. In Australia, the local government association is pressing for the federal governments and states to contribute funds to local governments for natural disaster mitigation. They also want local governments to budget natural disaster repair costs. Increasingly, the approach used to identify risks and contain recovery costs is ERM. ERM allows the organization to identify and prioritize the risks it faces. This allows for the efficient allocation of resources. ERM is also a positive contributor to the success of Smart City projects and the creation of resilience.

RISK	LIKELIHOOD	IMPACT	MITIGATION
Execution Risk: There is a lot of inter-depend-ence on multiple agencies during the implemen-tation of basic/core pro-ject components	**Low to Moderate:** The selected area has infrastruc-ture setup long ago, this cre-ates a more complex coordi-native problem	**Moderate:** Level of coordination required during execution of project would be high.	**Address:** Planned Coordi-nation, Commu-nication Partici-patory planning from project concept to im-plementation
Capacity Constraints: Implementation of Smart Project will require skills that are not available across various agen-cies.	**Low to Moderate:** Constraint to attracting talent as compensa-tion are not market driven.	**Moderate:** Moderate im-pact on infra-structure im-provement and utility opera-tion.	**Address:** Appoint Project Manager Consultant.

Table 1 - City of Vadodara Smart City Mitigation

The Virginia Beach case is a good example of the application of the IoT in a manner which cost effectively helps mitigate flood damage. The sensors provide the city with information which allows them to warn residents in the flooding areas 36 hours ahead of time. This provides individual households and neighborhoods time to evacuate or take additional actions to reduce flood damage. The information also allows the city to map in detail neighborhood flood information. Information which will allow the city to take neighborhood specific mitigative action.

The development of smart cites with systems capable of resisting attacks, requires long term thinking and an enterprise wide perspective. While the CIP report does not specify specific risk management principles, federal agencies are required by OMB Circular A-123 to implement Enterprise Risk Management (ERM). It is likely that the implementation guide, 'Playbook: Enterprise Risk Management for U.S. Federal Government', will provide these risk management principles. Such a linkage would be consistent with the desire to reduce the cost of natural disasters and increase organizational and community resilience.   ERM is becoming a minimum professional requirement for public sector managers.

KEY POINTS

- Cost of natural disasters is increasing.

- Number of natural disasters is increasing.

- FEMA is adopting a common risk vocabulary and risk metrics.

- NIST sees ERM as an important contributor to cyber-security.

- ERM approach is needed to deal with the multiple and ever increasingly costly risks.

- ERM is increasingly be adopted by government around the world.

- ERM helps improve operational efficiency.

- ERM is cost effective.

CHAPTER 2:
ENTERPRISE RISK MANAGEMENT IN THE PUBLIC SECTOR

INTRODUCTION

Having indicated why ERM is needed and its positive benefits, this chapter reviews the extent of ERM's adoption in the public sector and how higher levels of government are encouraging lower levels of governments to implement ERM.

CURRENT STATUS OF ERM

The exact number of governments worldwide that are implementing ERM is currently unknown. However, its use is widespread. ERM is mandated in South Africa and the United Kingdom. In Canada, the provinces of Novia Scotia, British Columbia and New Brunswick all have an ERM policy. The Commonwealth of Australia and the states of Victoria, Queensland, New South Wales and Western Australia have an ERM policy. In the United States (U.S.), the Office of Management and Budget (OMB), with the issuance of Circular A-123, mandated that all federal departments and agencies implement ERM. To assist with implementation, the Chief Financial Officers Council and Performance Improvement Council developed 'The Playbook: Implementing Enterprise Risk Management'.

The U.S. Congress mandated that all state Departments of Transportation include a risk asset management plan in their Transportation Asset Management Plan. Three states California, Tennessee and Washington have mandated ERM.

An exploratory examination of local government websites also shows significant penetration:

1. Canada, out of 79 government websites examined, 17% had an ERM policy

2. New Zealand, out of 15 websites examined, 33% had an ERM policy.

3. Australia, out of 77 websites examined, 32% had an ERM policy.

4. United States, out of 242 websites examined, 3% had some aspect of ERM.

ERM has penetrated deeply into the operational practice of commonwealth governments. With OMB's issuance of Circular A - 123, the United States at the federal level is catching up with foreign colleagues. However, local and state governments in the U.S., lag their foreign colleagues. But, with state departments of transportation under an ERM mandate, state level implementation of ERM will likely increase.

ERM'S ADOPTION IN THE UNITED STATES
Mandates are a very direct way of forcing ERM implementation. A more subtle encouragement is ERM's inclusion in guides and manuals. FEMA and NIST are adopting and promoting ERM in this way.

FEMA DISASTER RECOVER REFORM ACT 2018

In January 2018, Federal Emergency Management Agency posted 'Draft National Mitigation Investment Strategy'. One of the purposes of the strategy is to improve the coordination of risk management between and among federal, public, private, and non-profit sector entities. This is to be accomplished by:

- Developing a common vocabulary for understanding risk and mitigation.

- Developing common metrics for evaluating mitigation and resilience.

- Modifying federal processes to promote holistic approaches to risk management and mitigation planning.

- Incorporating evaluation of mitigation issues into continuous improvement processes. (1)

The strategic mitigation objectives are to develop a common risk management vocabulary, common metrics and the use of a holistic approach to risk management. This can only be accomplished by having all levels of governments use a common risk management approach. Since the Playbook is the federal guide to ERM, it is likely to be the basis for the vocabulary and holistic risk management approach. Lastly, there is the expectation that a proactive mitigative effort reduces costs.

In October 2018 President Trump signed the Disaster Recovery Reform Act. (2) It expands federal grant money for mitigative actions. For instance, it authorizes the National Public Infrastructure Pre-Disaster Hazard Mitigation Grant Program. The program focuses funds for infrastructure projects with the goal of increasing community resilience 'before a disaster occurs. With steady federal funding, it is hoped that state, local and tribal governments will improve resiliency by anticipating risk and developing mitigative efforts.

The act also requires FEMA to aid state and local governments with building code and floodplain management ordinance administration and enforcement. This is a clear recognition that changes in the administrative process need to occur. Further, the management of risk need to be proactive and not reactive.

NATIONAL INSTITUTE OF STANDARDS AND TECHNOLOGY – CYBER - SECURITY

The National Institute of Standards and Technology (NIST) is tasked with the responsibility of developing cyber-security procedures for federal agencies. In addition to their guide on cyber-security for federal agencies, NIST published a guide for all other organizations both public and private. It is entitled 'Cybersecurity is Everyone's Job'. The guide indicates that management should "regularly commission objective risk assessments of the organization." In addition, cyber risk should be included in the 'Enterprise Risk Management process'.

NIST recognizes that computers and network systems are so integrated into governmental operations, that cyber-security can no longer be isolated to the Information Technology department. Cyber-security must be a part of the broader organizational risk management process.

Cheryl McGrath, Vice President and General Manager of a Canadian Security Company makes this point as well. While her comment is directed at the private sector, it is equally applicable to the public sector:

"Rather than investing in new tools and programs simply to mitigate the latest threat or regulation in the headlines (the outside-in approach), a more sustainable and effective strategy is to first understand your specific enterprise risk, and then make security spending and staffing decisions accordingly (inside-out). Hurricanes are a horrible threat to houses, but if you use 'inside-out' thinking and understand that, in Canada, power outages and ice storms are far more likely risks to your house than hurricanes, you're going to invest in generators, not metal shutters for your windows. This same thinking needs to be brought to enterprise security." (3)

Given the U.S. government's adoption of ERM and its inclusion in NIST cyber-security, FEMA guides and the ERM mandate for state departments of transportation, it is worth examining how other governments have either mandated or pushed ERM to lower levels of government. Such an examination provides additional insights as to what might happen in the United States and in other countries where ERM is not being used by government.

ERM'S ADOPTION BY OTHER GOVERNMENTS

UNITED KINGDOM

In the United Kingdom, ERM is considered part of a good governance framework. The framework was developed by The Chartered Institute of Public Finance and Accountancy (CIPFA) and Society of Local Chief Executives (SOLACE). The framework was presented in a document entitled 'Delivering God Governance in Local Government Framework'. The framework has been adopted by the International Federation of Accountants (IFAC). The IFAC has members from 129 countries and represents 2.5 million accountants around the world. There are seven elements in the international framework. These are:

1. Strong commitment to integrity, ethical values, and the rule of law.

2. Openness and comprehensive stakeholder engagement.

3. Defining outcomes in terms of sustainable economic, social and environment benefits.

4. Determining the interventions necessary to optimize the achievement of intended outcomes.

5. Developing the capacity of the entity, including the capability of its leadership and the individuals within it.

6. Managing risk and performance through robust internal control and strong public financial management.

7. Implementing good practice in transparency and reporting to deliver effective accountability.

EFFECTIVE RISK MANAGEMENT

The international framework indicates that risk management and internal controls are integral parts of the organization performance measurement system. The elements of an effective risk management system are consistent with international standards, such as ISO 31000:2018. According to the framework, effective risk management should include:

1. Implementing a risk management framework.

2. Defining the entity's risk management strategy, approving the limits for risk taking, where feasible, and

determining the criteria for internal control.

3. Integrating the processes for managing risk into the entity's overall governance, strategy and planning, management, reporting processes, policies, values and culture.

4. Reviewing key strategic, operational, financial and fraud risks regularly and division responses consistent with achieving the organization's objectives and outcomes.

5. Engaging staff in all aspects of the risk management process.

6. Monitoring and reviewing the risk management framework and processes on the regular basis. (4)

In 2016, CIPFA and SOLACE issued an update to 'Delivering Good Governance in Local Government: Framework'. This framework is to be used by local governments in conducting and reporting an annual governance statement. With the issuance of the update, the framework's elements became an audit standard and annual requirement.

This mandate, unlike one's which are legislated by higher levels of government, was developed by two professional organizations. One was the Charter Accountants Association. The other was Society of Local Chief Executives. The basic framework was picked up by the International Federation of Accountants. The federation spread the framework internationally. The framework and ERM are internationally considered best practices.

AUSTRALIAN COMMONWEALTH

The Commonwealth of Australia provides another model. In Australia, The Public Governance, Performance and Accountability Act (PGPAA) 2013 was passed. It outlines the risk management obligations of

Australian governments. The Act specifies that Australia governments must establish and maintain an:

- Appropriate system of risk oversight and management for the entity.

- Appropriate system of internal controls for the entity. (5)

The aim of Act and the accompanying ERM policy is to ensure that governments in Australia make informed decisions with respect to the activities that they undertake, by appropriately considering both risks and opportunities.

In 2014, ERM was mandated for all Commonwealth departments and agencies. In this respect, the Australian Commonwealth is like the U.S. federal government's in its ERM implementation and stress on risk mitigation. It just started a year earlier.

NEW SOUTH WALES AUSTRALIA

Despite having an ERM requirement in an accountability act, as the data in Chapter 2 indicates, not all states or local governments have implemented ERM. Thus, ERM is unevenly applied.

One state which has adopted ERM and is aggressive in promoting ERM to local governments is New South Wales (NSW). Its local government department assists local government with the implementation of better practices. One of its tools is a self-assessment check list. The items in the check list represent better practice. The check list includes an ERM component.

Check List

The check list is divided into specific performance areas. Each area has performance related questions which are to be check off. For instance, the Risk Management section asks:

1. Does council have a risk management plan that addresses all key business risks facing council?

2. How was the risk management plan prepared?

3. Has council assigned responsibility across the organisation for implementation of the risk management plan?

4. How does council monitor risk management plan and progress against risk management strategies? (6)

ERM Better Practice Impact

Local governments can use the check list to determine areas of better practice deficiencies. The check list is also used when local government staff conduct on site audits. The effectiveness of its efforts to push ERM to lower levels of government can be seen in the number of local governments with an ERM policy. Of 102 local government websites examined 39% had an ERM policy. (The 102 local governments represent about 95% of the local governments in NSW.) That is 7% higher than the general Australian local government use. NSW's effort to push ERM to local levels of government appears to be having a positive impact.

Mandate or Encourage?

Either approach, whether driven by professional associations or through technical assistance from national or state government, could be used to facilitate ERM's spread in the United States and elsewhere. Given that ERM is being used at the federal level, it seems more likely that the U.S. federal government will act more as a model and encourage ERM by incorporating its use in grants and guidelines.

However, given that Congress has mandated that state departments of transportation must conduct risk assessment, if the costs of natural disasters, cyber-attacks or other risks continue to rise, or it looks like these costs or the lack of risk management might threaten national security, it is possible Congress might expand the mandate.

SUMMARY

With the costs of natural disasters rising, the U.S. federal government is increasingly emphasizing ERM. Not only has the U.S. federal government adopted ERM, Congress has mandated that state departments of transportation implement ERM. ERM is also being emphasized by FEMA and NIST. In both cases, ERM is seen as a way of improving municipal resilience and help mitigate the damage of cyberattacks.

Elsewhere in the world, ERM has penetrated administrative practice in Australia, Canada, New Zealand, South Africa and the United Kingdom. The model used by many of these governments is ISO 31000. ISO 31000 is one of two international ERM standards.

Finally, ERM is increasingly seen as a minimum competency for public sector managers.

KEY POINTS

- ERM is a considered a best practice in the United Kingdom and by the International Federation of Accountants.

- Australian Commonwealth and several Australian states are modeling ERM.

- In New South Wales, ERM is being promoted by the state's Local Government Department through the provision of technical assistance and performance audits.

- United States Congress has mandated that state departments of transportation implement ERM.

- If the costs of natural disasters continue to rise and voluntary mitigative action is not taken, it is possible that the U.S. Congress will mandate ERM's implementation.

CHAPTER 3:

RISK MANAGEMENT MODELS

INTRODUCTION

This book is about implementing ISO 31000 in government. However, because ISO 31000 is one of two international ERM standards and both models are being used worldwide, a brief discussion of the other model, COSO ERM, and a comparison with ISO 31000:2018 is appropriate.

COSO ERM - TREADWAY COMMISSION

The Committee of Sponsoring Organizations (COSO) was formed in 1985. The sponsoring organizations are American Accounting Association, American Institute of Certified Public Accountants, Financial Executive International, the Institute of Management Accountants and the Institute of Internal Auditors.

The goal of the commission was to provide guidance to executive management and governance bodies on business ethics, internal control, Enterprise Risk Management, fraud and financial reporting. The Treadway Commission issued a report entitled 'Internal Control – Integrated Framework' in 1992. It was later updated with minor changes in 1994.

RISK CONCERNS

In 2004, COSO published 'Enterprise Risk Management – Integrated Framework' (COSO ERM). The report was in response to increasing concerns with the cost of risk events and their ability to hinder the accomplishment of an organization's mission. The publication expanded the internal control framework by focusing on Enterprise Risk Management.

The revision expresses the growing concerns about the risks an organization faces. The report notes:

> "Organizations encounter challenges that impact reliability, relevancy, and trust. Stakeholders are more engaged today, seeking greater transparency and accountability for managing the impact of risk while also critically evaluating leadership's ability to crystalize opportunities. Even success can bring with it additional downside risk - the risk of not being able to fulfill unexpectedly high demand, or maintain expected business momentum, for example. (1)

2017 REVISION

In June 2017, COSO issued another revision entitled 'Risk Management Integrating with Strategy and Performance'. The revision is designed to recognize and help organizations adapt to a complex and volatile global environment by improving their ability to recognize and deal with risk. One goal is to protect value.

> "Value is eroded when management implements strategies, or takes actions, which do not yield expected outcomes or fails to execute day to day tasks." (2)

ERM, protects value by providing management with information which helps them make better decisions. These decisions are to be based on an assessment of risks that could prevent the accomplishment of their mission. At the same time, it improves resource utilization and enhances organizational resilience.

In the public-sector, value is not a term often used. Yet, when public services are discussed, different words, like 'customer satisfaction' and 'responding to need' or 'needed or necessary services' are used. In the United Kingdom, value is associated with 'Value for Money' or efficiency.

COSO MAJOR COMPONENTS

COSO ERM is based on five components. The components provide the framework within which the ERM process takes place. The components are designed to help fully integrate ERM into the organization's culture and administrative processes. The components are listed below.

The five components are:

- **Governance and Culture:** Governance sets the organization's tone and reinforces the importance of establishing oversights responsibilities. Culture is the organization's ethical values, desired behaviour and understanding of risk.

- **Strategy and Objective-Setting:** Strategy is the long-term organizational plan, which includes objectives for accomplishing this strategy. ERM and strategy and objective-setting work together in the strategic-planning process. Part of this process is for the governing body and management to state their risk appetite. The risk appetite is the degree of pain the organization is willing to suffer for each risk. Once the risk appetite is established, strategic and operational objectives can be put in place.

- **Performance:** Risks that can impact strategic and business objectives are identified. Risks are prioritized by their probability of occurrence and severity. The results are reported to key risk stakeholders.

- **Review and Revision:** Risks, their prioritization, and the mitigation (treatment) efforts are continually assessed to determine how to manage ERM components over time.

- **Information, Communication and Reporting:** Information on risks and their prioritization is continually gathered from both internal and external sources and shared throughout the organization. (3)

INTERRELATIONSHIP BETWEEN STEPS

In addition to the components, COSO ERM lists six process steps and various actions linked to each step. The relationship between the steps and associated actions can be seen in Table 2.

While the verbiage is different, at its core, COSO ERM is consistent with the ISO 31000:2018 philosophy and goals. What differentiates ISO 31000:2018 from COSO ERM is the level of detail that COSO ERM provides with respect to the linkage between the steps in the risk assessment methodology and the various tools available for use.

PROCESS	INPUTS	TYPES OF APPROACH	OUTPUTS
Risk Identification	Strategy and objectives Risk appetite and acceptable variation in performance	Data tracking Interviews Facilitated workshops Question-naires/surveys Process analysis Leading indica-tors	Risk Universe
Assessment	Risk universe Risk severity measures	Probabilistic modeling Non-probabilis-tic modeling (sensitivity anal-ysis) Judgmental evaluation Benchmarking Heat Map	Risk assessment results
Prioritizing risk	Prioritized risk assessment results Prioritization criteria	Judgmental evaluations Quantitative scoring meth-ods	Prioritized risk assessment results
Responding to risk	Prioritized risk assessment results	Risk profile templates or pro forma risk profiles Cost Benefit Analysis	Develop risk re-sponse Residual risk as-sessment results
Developing a portfolio view	Residual risk as-sessment	Judgmental evaluations	Portfolio view of risk

	results	Quantitative scoring methods	
Monitoring per-formance	Residual risk assessment results	Dashboards Performance Reports	Corrective actions

Table 2 - Relationship of ERM Steps (4)

ENVIRONMENTAL, SOCIAL AND GOVERNANCE

In 2018, COSO in conjunction with the World Business Council for Sustainable Development, published a supplement to COSO ERM. It is entitled 'Enterprise Risk Management: Applying Enterprise Risk Management to Environmental, Social and Governance-related risks.'

The supplement "addresses an increasing need for companies to integrate Environmental, Social and Governance (ESG) - relate risks into their ERM process". The ESG's are consistent with those identified in the Lloyd's of London Cities at Risk study and those risks listed in chapter 1. The supplement states:

> "Leveraging a company's enterprise risk (ERM) governance and processes can support identification, assessment and mitigation of ESG-related risks at an enterprise level." (5)

In a side bar, the document states: "Both COSO and WBCSD believe that Enterprise Risk Management is the most powerful conduit to address ESG-related risks." (6)

While the supplement is geared towards the private sector, it clearly shows that all organizations, whether private or public face similar risks. The supplement also shows that the private sector sees ERM as the 'most powerful conduit' to deal with what they term ESG-related risks.

This is a view the International Organization for Standardization (ISO) shares. Although, it is not as explicit in identifying ESG-related risks.

ISO 31000:2018 STANDARD

ISO is the International Organization for Standardization. It is an organization which establishes internationally recognized standards for the certification of specific activities and organizational processes. Its certification standards cover a wide variety of economic activities and products, from medical devices to cyber security. One of their standards is for Enterprise Risk Management. It is designated ISO 31000.

In 2018, ISO updated ISO 31000. The revised standard emphasizes two elements. The first is ERM's contribution to organizational value through integration into the organizations daily processes. The second is involvement of senior management and the governing body.

VALUE CREATION AND PROTECTION
Value creation and protection are the result of following eight principles. The steps are listed below:

1. **Integrated:** Risk management becomes a standard part of all operational activities.

2. **Structured and Comprehensive:** A structured and comprehensive approach to risk management contributes to consistent and comparable results.

3. **Customized:** The risk management process can be scaled for any level within the organization, from the strategic to the project level.

4. **Inclusive:** Involvement of stakeholders allows their views and

perceptions to be considered.

5. **Dynamic:** Risks can arise and decline as the environment changes. Risk management anticipates and responses to these changes.

6. **Best Available Information:** The best available information is used to assess risks. This includes historical and current information and considers any limitation or uncertainty with regards to information.

7. **Human and Cultural Factors:** Human behaviour and organizational culture are considered when developing risk management strategy.

8. **Continual Improvement:** Risk management strategies continual to evolve as new risks are identified and other risks are dropped. (7)

Despite the different vocabulary, both COSO ERM and ISO 3100:2018, have a consistent approach to risk management. Further, by implementing ERM and integrating it into the organization's processes, both recognize that ERM protects value.

Value can be expressed in several ways. The first is the avoidance of risk events through the identification of these events and development of a mitigation (treatment) strategy. The second is through increased efficiencies.

RISK AVOIDANCE

The ability to anticipate and avoid or mitigate the adverse impact of risks is accomplished by implementing ERM.

EFFICIENCY IMPROVEMENT

Efficiency improvements are accomplished by customizing the ERM process to the organizational level, continual monitoring of the risks and the mitigation strategies and adjusting when needed.

MODEL SIMILARITIES

The 2017 COSO ERM revision and the 2018 revision of ISO 31000 move the two models closer. Both now stress the need for upper management's and the governing body's involvement. This emphasis is made because it is realized that without their overt support, the integration of ERM into all operational activities will be incomplete at best. Further, without their active support, ERM will be still born.

There is another similarity between the two models. That is the way they view risks.

BOTH MODELS ARE OBJECTIVE BASED

There are two approaches to assessing and describing risks. One is event based. The other is objective based. An event based approach describes the risk as an individual occurrence within a specific time span. The event, a flood, is generally expressed in terms of years between events. A flood, using this approach, would be termed a 100-year flood.

The second approach is objective based. An objective based approach looks at both the probability of occurrence and the potential negative impact of the risk on the organization's ability to accomplish it mission.

By taking an objective based approach, all risks are assessed in part based on the probability of occurrence in the current year. A probability of occurrence of a hundred-year flood would be 1%, while a five-year event would be 20%. Thus, there is a common measure for each risk. A measure that when combined with the estimated impact, allows for the prioritization of the risks in a systematic manner.

OBJECTIVE BASED APPROACH BECOMING DOMINANT

The objective approach is becoming increasingly necessary because of the frequency and intensity of natural disasters and other risks. It is necessary for two reasons. The first is psychological. When an event is classified as a 100-year event, decision makers feel that unless they are 99 years from the last event, or seemingly one year away from the next event, there is no need to worry. When faced with multiple demands for resources, it is too easy to ignore risks deemed years away.

The second reason is that risk events are occurring more frequently. For instance, New York City is experiencing a flood every five years instead of every 500. Using the objective based approach, the risk would be rated .2% for a 500-year event, (6) as opposed to a rating of 20% for one every five years.

By using a common measure which is based on the probability of the event occurring each year, management can better assess the risks the organization faces. When the probability of occurrence is combined with the adverse impact, all the risk an organization faces can be prioritized. Once prioritized, mitigative efforts and the organization's risk management strategy can be determined.

INNOVATION AND RISK AVOIDANCE

Both ISO 31000 and COSO ERM note that to be innovative an organization must often take risks. While both focus on reducing the adverse impact, both stress that the risk appetite of the organization will determine the amount of risk the governing body and management find acceptable. Neither model does a good job of providing a good discussion of the linkage between innovation and risk. Consequently, it is worth looking at another model which formally combines innovation and risk management. That model is the United States Baldrige 'Performance Excellence Framework'.

BALDRIGE FRAMEWORK

In 2017 ERM was added to the framework. Two years earlier, innovation had been added. Innovation according to the Baldrige Framework is "making meaningful change to improve organization products, services, programs, processes, and operations" with goal of creating value and improving services and operations. (8)

> "Innovation should be integrated into daily works and be supported by your performance improvement system. Systematic process for identifying strategic opportunities should reach across your entire organization and should explore strategic alliances with complementary organizations." (9)

With respect to risk the framework suggest that the organization be managed in a way such that identifying innovative opportunities are evaluated in relation to intelligent risks. Intelligent risks are defined as: "Opportunities for which the potential gain outweighs the potential harm or loss to your organization's future success." The degree of risk that is 'intelligent' is the tolerance (risk appetite) for failure versus success.

In sum for an organization to be innovative and effective, risk management and innovation must become part of the organization's culture. Innovative strategies need to be assessed against the organization's risk appetite.

However, it must be recognized that innovation can take many forms. EPB of Chattanooga and Virginia Beach StormSense show how organizations are using the IoT to be innovative. But sometimes, it is merely the application of existing administrative processes in a slightly different way. The City of Oshawa Canada provides such an example.

CITY OF OSHAWA CANADA – CASE STUDY (10)

The City Manager of Oshawa Canada, in the 2017 Corporate Risk Management Policy and Procedure memo, states:

> "Risk management is required for good corporate governance and is an integral component of the City's continuous improvement framework. It is therefore important to understand risk and ensure it is managed."

The purpose of a Corporate Risk Management Policy and Procedure is to embed a systematic approach to identify, assess, mitigate, monitor and report on risks that impact the City's existing functions and processes. The goal is to incorporate risk management into everyday activities, allow for a planned and consistent approach to reducing the impact and likelihood of an adverse event and increase the possibility and magnitude of benefits that could result from seizing an opportunity.

In 2010, city staff asked the auditor how to improve risk management. The city implemented ERM in 2011. The first step was to have city departments developed risk registers. A risk register is a formal document which lists the prioritized risks and the mitigative actions. In 2014, departments reported back with their risk registers.

In 2015, the ERM process was reviewed to:

- Better enable the city to achieve its strategic goals.
- Strengthen planning, priority-setting and decision making.
- Better manage risks and advance opportunities.
- Allocate resources to high-risk areas.
- Clarify responsibility and accountability for risk management.

The review resulted in senior management being more engaged with ERM and the development of a set of principles to guide the ERM process.

Risk management is an essential component of good governance practices. Good decisions are made when supported by a systematic approach to risk management. Risk management is integrated into strategic and business planning.

Integration of risk management within the city is supported by corporate values that encourage everyone to identify and manage risk. Significant risks should be disclosed when reporting to management, Council or Standing Committees.

To integrate ERM into city activities and encourage continual improvement, the city grouped four activities into a Continuous Improvement Framework. The activities are:

- **Lean Initiatives:** Use teams to identify ways the city can improve services and reduce costs. From 2014 to 2017 teams completed 32 projects which improved efficiency and reduced costs.

- **Service Project Reviews:** Like lean initiative teams, but without the formalities.

- **Audits:** Internal Audits are used to identify areas for improvement and ensure compliance with laws, rules and regulations.

- **ERM:** A risk management methodology is used to identify, prioritized and mitigate risks.

Two examples demonstrate the interrelationship between the continuous improvement activities. An audit of overtime expenditures determined the city did not have an overtime tracking procedure. The auditor recommended that a lean initiative team develop an overtime tracking procedure and examine processes to reduce over time.

A second example is the use of the ERM risk scores to prioritize the annual audit. Below are areas included in the 2018 audit plan with their risk ratings.

- Health and Safety   High
- Fleet Management   Medium
- Real Estate   Medium
- Absence Management   High
- Workforce productivity data   High

DEFINITIONS

Below are the definitions of a few word which are key to understanding ISO 31000:2018.

- **Context:** Environment in which the organization operates.

- **Inherent Risk:** The probability of loss arising out of circumstances or existing in an environment in the absence of any action to control or modify the circumstances.

- **Level of Risk:** Magnitude of risk is expressed in terms of likelihood and consequence.

- **Likelihood:** Possibility or chance of something occurring or happening. Likelihood is also called probability or frequency.

- **Operational Risk:** Potential of loss attributable to process variation or disruption in its operations caused by internal or external factors.

- **Reputational Risk:** Decrease in brand equity or credibility of the organization.

- **Residual Risk:** Risk remaining after risk treatment. Residual risk can contain unidentified risk. Residual risk is also called retained risk. Exposure to loss remaining after other known risks have been countered, factored in, or eliminated.

- **Risk:** Uncertainty on achieving a business objective. Risk is also a deviation from an objective, which can be either be positive or negative. Objectives can be from the financial, quality, project, process, program, transactional, or supply chain.

- **Risk Analysis:** Process to understand the nature of risk and to determine the level of risk. Risk analysis is the basis for risk evaluation and decisions about risk treatment and risk management.

- **Risk Aversion:** Attitude and policy to move away and not pursue opportunities and actions.

- **Risk Management:** Coordinated activities to direct and control an organization's risk

- **Risk Management Framework:** Set of components that

provide the foundations and organizational arrangement for designing, implementing, monitoring, reviewing and continually improving risk management throughout the organization.

- **Risk Management Policy:** Statement of the overall intentions and direction of an organization related to risk management.

- **Risk Appetite:** Level of risk that an organization is prepared to accept, before action is deemed necessary to reduce it, sometimes called risk tolerance.

- **Risk Attitude:** Organization's approach to assess and eventually pursue, retain, take or turn away from risk.

- **Scope:** Legal, geographic, and mission boundaries that the organization must adhere to.

- **VUCA**: Short for **V**olatility, **U**ncertainty, **C**omplexity and **A**mbiguity. It is used by the private sector and military to describe a complex interrelated and dynamic environment. The interrelationship and dynamic nature of the interconnected environment adds complexity and ambiguity.

SUMMARY

There are two dominant international ERM models. One is COSO ERM. The other is ISO 31000:2018. Both models have similar steps although they use different terminology. The COSO ERM steps are: Risk Identification, Risk Assessment, Prioritize Risk, Respond to Risk, Develop a Portfolio, and Monitor. These are steps like those in ISO 31000:2018. (The specific ISO 31000:2018 steps will be discussed in subsequent chapters.)

Other similarities between the two models is the emphasis on the involvement of upper level management and the governing body. Both models also stress the need for innovation and the managing of the risks associated with such efforts.

KEY POINTS

- ERM model used most frequently by government is ISO 31000.

- ISO 31000 is one of two dominate international ERM models.

- ISO 31000 was revised in 2018.

- COSO ERM and ISO 31000:2018 stress value protection.

- COSO ERM and ISO 31000:2018 stress management and governing body involvement.

- COSO ERM and ISO 31000:2018 also stress innovation.

CHAPTER 4:
ERM IN ORGANIZATIONAL CULTURE

INTRODUCTION

As noted in Chapter 1, ISO 31000 is an international standard for addressing the risks an organization faces. To address these risks effectively and continually, the risk management methodology needs to be integrated into the organization's operations. Risk Management must become part of the organization's culture. This is fundamental precept to ISO 31000.

ORGANIZATIONAL CULTURE

The Northumberland County Council of the United Kingdom notes:

> "Effective risk management will assist the organization in the achievement of its objectives, through the identification and treatment of factors which could prevent their accomplishment. It forms an essential element of the provision of an efficient and effective service to the public." (1)

Not long ago, the author had a meeting with the Chief Administrative Officer (CAO) of a large municipality. The municipality is in the early stage of ERM implementation.

The CAO had visited Edmonton Canada to determine how a large city had implemented ERM. After the visit, he formed a risk management team composed of top department heads. Discussions with the City Council about ERM implementation also occurred. Currently, the ERM implementation process is on hold, while the city revises its budget process.

This is an example of how easy it is for the ERM process to be delayed or stopped. There is always a reason for not accepting that an organization faces risks that need to be managed. Such reasons, and most are valid, include: "We do not have the time to implement something new. No one else is doing it. It does not pay for itself."

It has been shown that ERM contributes substantially to the organization, both in return on investment and efficiency improvements. But to maximize ERM's benefits, it must be implemented and become part of the organization's culture.

ERM PREPARATION
Appendix A provides a series of questions which allow management to assess how effective it is in ensuring that ERM will become part of the organization's culture. The questions also provide a guide on how to implement ERM and begin the integration process.

There are four preparatory questions that need to be asked. The answer to these questions ensures the successful implementation of ERM.

1. Does the agency have an explicitly stated risk management policy that complements its vision and strategic objectives?

2. Does the agency have an explicit risk management appetite?

3. Has the governing body developed and implemented a robust risk management framework appropriate to the size of the agency?

4. What administrative structure is the organization going to use to implement ERM?

These are questions which upper level management and the governing body need to answer. With the 2018 revision of ISO 31000, the governing body's responsibilities have been increased.

GOVERNING BODY RESPONSIBILITY

The governing body is expected to take an active part in the risk management process by:

* Ensuring that risks are adequately considered when setting the organization's objectives.

* Understanding the principal risks that could prevent the organization from accomplishing its mission and established goals.

* Ensuring that risk mitigation is implemented and operating effectively.

* Ensuring that such risks are appropriate to the organization's context and objectives.

* Ensuring that information about the organization's risks and mitigative activities is reported regularly to the governing body.

Without the support and active involvement of the governing body, ERM will not become fully integrated into the decision-making process. The governing body must both understand and embrace ERM.

Management, pushed in multiple directions and facing other priorities, will generally be slow to implement ERM, if not dismiss it all together. Since the governing body sets the agenda for the organization, their involvement is necessary to provide direction and a prod. The governing body also acts as a link between the citizenry and management. Therefore, it is necessary that it be kept fully informed of the risks the organization faces and the mitigative actions. It must also be a full participant in developing the organization's risk management strategy.

RISK MANAGEMENT POLICY

One of the most important documents that the governing body must approve is the Risk Management Policy. The policy complements the strategic vision.

RAMOTSHERE MOILA LOCAL MUNICIPALITY SOUTH AFRICA

The Ramotshere Moila Local Municipality of South Africa risk management policy indicates the commitment to managing risk. The risk management process is to be integrated into the organization's administrative processes. It also indicates that risks are to be prioritized based on their adverse impact on achievement of strategic and business objectives

RISK APPETITE

While ISO mentions the need for the development of an organizational risk appetite, it does not indicate who is responsible for

Ramotshere Moila Local Municipality Risk Management Policy (2)

The Ramotshere Moiloa Local Municipality (RMLM) strives to proactively take initiative in seizing opportunities and developing solutions in line with our strategic and business objectives. We recognise that in doing so, we may accept risks in order to create value for our stakeholders, including employees and the general public.

In this context, risk is defined as the uncertainty of future events that could adversely influence the achievement of our strategic and business objectives. It is for this reason that risk management is viewed as a process which is used by all levels of management throughout the municipality to identify, evaluate, treat, monitor and report risks to ensure the achievement of the municipality's objectives. The policy should clearly state the organization's commitment ERM and its intent to integrate it throughout the organization. The risk management policy for the Ramotshere Moila Local Municipality of South Africa is shown below.

developing and approving the risk appetite. Generally, it is the responsibility of both management and the governing body.

The risk appetite is the amount of risk that management is prepared to accept or avoid. The risk appetite provides a connection between risk and organizational activities. The risk appetite must be determined at the highest levels of the organization because it focuses the mitigative actions needed to implement the risk management strategy.

PRACTICAL TIPS: DEVELOPING A RISK MANAGEMENT POLICY

- Tailor it to the organization's context.
- State the rationale for managing risk.
- Illustrate the connections between the organization's objectives and other relevant policies.
- Define accountabilities and responsibilities for managing risk.
- Identify the human resources and systems required to manage risk.
- Describe how risk management performance will be measured and reported.
- Specify how the risk management framework will be reviewed.
- Provide a provision for how risks will be escalated.
- Include how the policy will be communicated and reinforced.

WORCESTER SHIRE COUNCIL

The Worcester Shire Council of the UK notes:

> "The purpose of risk appetite is to set out an organisation's attitude to risk and to provide consistency in the decision-making process. Risk appetite enables well-measured risk-taking that will lead to improved service delivery. In addition, it will help to identify when a more cautious approach should be taken to mitigate threats." (3)

Below are some basic questions that help determine the risk appetite. The risk appetite levels are generally Low, Medium, and High. Although, the determination of the levels is made at the highest level in the organization. The risk appetite needs to be designed to communicate to a broad spectrum of stakeholders – employees, citizens, press, any regulatory bodies etc. It must clearly state how acceptable any risk is to management and the governing body.

Appetite Levels	Description
Averse (Low)	Avoidance of risk and uncertainty.
Minimalist (Medium Low)	Preference for ultra-safe options that have a low degree of risk and only have a potential for limited reward.
Cautious (Medium)	Preference for safe options that have a low degree of risk and may only have limited potential for reward.
Open (Medium High)	Willing to consider all options and choose the one that is most likely to result in successful delivery while also providing an acceptable level of reward.
Hungry (High)	Eager to be innovative and to choose options based on potential higher rewards (despite greater inherent risk).

Table 3- Risk Appetite for the Worcester Shire Council (4)

The risk appetite level is a key ingredient in determining the amount of mitigative activity to be taken to manage the risk. A low-level means that there is a low or little tolerance for risk. A low tolerance indicates that considerable effort must be exerted to manage the risk. The risk must be eliminated or substantively reduced. A high-level means there is great deal of tolerance. Thus, the risk can be accepted with no or little mitigative efforts. Table 3 shows the risk appetite of Worcester Shire Council UK.

The Worcester Shire Council has broken their risk appetite into five gradients. As noted earlier, many governments prefer to use only three. Further, some governments add greater detail to the description. For instance, under low tolerance it may be noted that the

---

PRACTICAL TIPS: QUESTIONS TO ASK WHEN DEVELOPING THE RISK APPETITE

- What does risk appetite mean for your agency?
- Why would risk appetite add value?
- Who needs to set the expectations and accountability?
- How can it be included into the governance, framework and process?
- When should decisions about risk appetite be made and communicated?

---

organization has "no tolerance for actions which adversely impact its reputation, and financial or legal liability, which includes fraud and stealing." While under Medium tolerance it states: "it has medium tolerance for honest mistakes and unsuccessful efforts to enhance innovation and revenue." High tolerance may be expressed as the "organization has a high tolerance for efficiency, revenue enhancement improvement and innovation." In other words, it is recognized that innovative activities have risks, the adverse impact of such risks are acceptable if the objective is efficiency improvements, revenue enhancement and innovation.

AMOUNT OF DETAIL

While the appetite level is flexible, as is the amount of detail provided in the description, it must be remembered that the risk appetite identification is fundamental to the ERM process. First, it communicates to the organization's stakeholders the boundaries with respect to risk taking. Second, it lays the foundation for the organization's risk management strategy. This is because it established the tolerance boundaries for specific risks and thereby informs the mitigative efforts.

RISK MANAGEMENT FRAMEWORK

The organization's risk management framework is the document which lays out the organization's ERM implementation process. It is essentially, like this book, a how to guide. It guides the organization through the sequences of the steps to be used to implement the process. Below is the executive summary for the Greater Geraldton City Council in Australia. It provides an overview of the Council's risk management effort.

GREATER GERALDRON CITY COUNCIL
To achieve the City of Greater Geraldton (City) agreed objectives and outcomes, the following Enterprise Wide Risk Management framework was adopted:

"The City will manage risk in accordance with the Australian/New Zealand Standard (AS/NZS ISO 31000:2009) risk management principles:

1. Maintain the highest possible integrity for services provided by the City of Greater Geraldton.

2. Safeguard the City of Greater Geraldton's physical and non-physical assets including employees, Councillors & Mayor financial and property (both physical and intellectual).

3. Create an environment where all employees will assume responsibility for managing risk.

4. Achieve and maintain legislative and regulatory compliance, professional standards and codes of conduct based on the best available information.

5. Ensure resources and operational capabilities are identified

and responsibility for managing risk allocated.

6. Demonstrate transparent and responsible risk management processes which align with accepted best practice through the implementation of a comprehensive risk management process which addresses uncertainty and the nature of that uncertainty together with continuous improvement of the process."(5)

This framework provides a basis for corporate and operational planning. It helps minimize costly surprises and leads to program efficiency and effectiveness. All of this enhances the delivery of services to the community.

The framework has two distinct components:

1. "Overview of the City's Strategic Enterprise Wide Risk Management Framework is provided. This maps the City's approach and the structures and processes that support an integrated risk management environment which links business objectives, risk, and related controls.

2. It sets out the specific processes associated with risk management activities within the City. It facilitates the preparation and documentation of comprehensive risk management plans to enable implementation of risk management practices across the City." (6)

As the executive summary indicates, the purpose of the ERM process is 'to create an environment' which will encourage all employees to manage the organization's risk. Such action will help the organization to allocate its resources in an efficient and effective manner. Finally, it will enhance the organization's decision making by integrating the ERM process into the organizations operating processes and strategic plan.

The risk management policy, the risk appetite and the risk management framework are the policy basis for the organization's ERM process. The policy and the appetite provide the boundaries for the ERM process. The framework is the implementation guide. It is to be used by all members of the organization as they evaluate the risks and develop mitigative actions, which protect resources and allow the organization to become more resilient.

The ERM policy and risk appetite are stressed in the guide and are based on ISO 31000:2018. What has not been stressed in either COSO ERM and ISO 31000:2018 is the administrative structure that helps ensure that ERM is integrated into the organization's processes. It is fine to say the governing body and upper level management need to be involved, but someone must carry out the steps in the ERM process. That someone is identified by the ERM administrative structure.

ORGANIZATIONAL STRUCTURE

Below are two examples of an administrative structure. One is that recommended in the Enterprise Risk Management Playbook. The other is the one used by the City of Windsor Canada.

The key difference is the present of Chief Risk Officer (CRO), who acts as the focal point and coordinator for ERM.

U.S. GOVERNMENT ERM ADMINISTRATIVE STRUCTURE

The Playbook requires an administrative structure to implement the ERM management process. The ERM process is overseen by a Risk Management Council (RMC). The RMC is responsible for the implementation and monitoring of department performance. The RMC consists of Senior Managers including the Chief Financial Officer, Chief Human Capital Officer, Chief Information Office, Chief Information

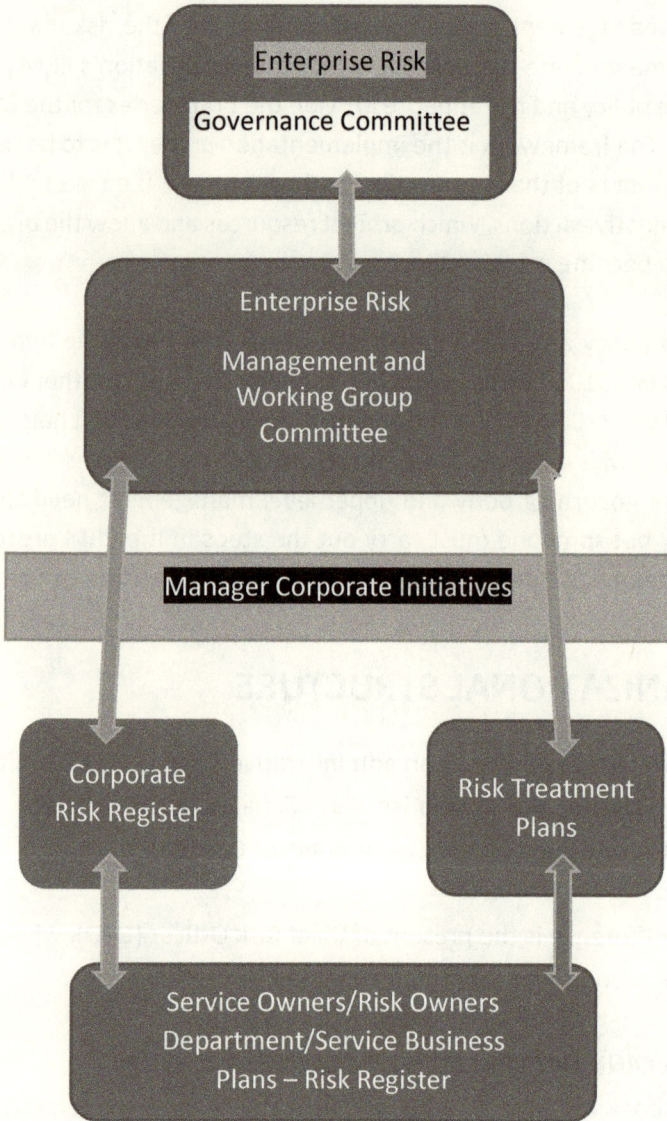

Figure 1 – City of Windsor Risk Management Structure

Security Officer, Designated Agency Ethics Official, Performance Improvement Officers and the CRO.

CHIEF RISK OFFICER

The CRO is the 'risk champion' and senior advisor for the agency. The CRO works with business unit managers to identify risk issues in a timely manner. This allows manager to take mitigative action appropriate to the level of risk.

The CRO is responsible for:

- Helping senior management develop and implement core policies with respect to risk management.

- Ensuring current risk levels and processes are consistent with risk policies.

- Supporting implementation of effective controls.

Developing strong reporting systems and analysis that incorporate quantitative and qualitative information to provide effective organization-wide views of risk.

- Identifying emerging risks and other situations that should be properly assessed.

The RMC is replicated in department and business units. The CRO works with the department and business unit teams and management. The CRO coordinates the risk identification and mitigation efforts and takes them to the corporate RMC.

CITY OF WINDSOR CANADA

Figure 1 is the governance structure guide used by the City of Windsor Canada. It is an extract from the city's Risk Management Framework.

The structure "assist senior management in ensuring appropriate management and mitigation of significant risks." (7)

The following roles and responsibilities support the City of Windsor ERM governance structure.

Enterprise Risk Management Governance Committee – Acts as a Steering Committee for the Enterprise Risk Management framework by providing support and direction to achieve the Corporate Enterprise Risk Management Strategy. The Committee will be comprised of the Chief Administrative Officer and the Corporate Leadership Team.

Their responsibilities are to:

- Review reports from the Enterprise Risk Management Working Committee and provide direction accordingly.

- Provide direction for significant and critical risks elevated to the Committee and/or refer to the Council.

- Perform annual review of enterprise risks.

- Approve changes, as necessary, to the Enterprise Risk Management framework, risk measurement criteria, risk universe and definitions, and governance structure.

The Enterprise Risk Management Working Committee reviews the significant and critical risks from a corporate perspective. The Committee is chaired by the Manager of the Corporate Initiatives. Its responsibilities are to:

- Review the Corporate Risk Register and risk treatment plans for significant and critical risks; and recommend further actions to mitigate risks, if necessary.

- Provide quarterly reports (or as deemed necessary) to the Enterprise Risk Governance Committee regarding the Corporation's risks and identify risk owners.

- Elevate significant and critical risks, as necessary, to the Enterprise Risk Governance Committee for direction/action.

- Develop procedures to ensure effective implementation of this framework.

As Manager of Corporate Initiatives, it manages the Enterprise Risk Management framework. This includes developing the Enterprise Risk Management framework to support the Corporation's Enterprise Risk Management strategy, implementing and monitoring the elements of the framework, and continuously improving the elements of the framework as required. Its responsibilities are to:

- Provide training on the ERM framework & its processes.

- Facilitate risk assessments as directed.

- Manage the Corporate risk register, which includes significant & critical risks.

- Monitor risk treatment plans that mitigate significant & critical risks.

- Assist in elevating significant & critical risks upward for direction/action.

Service Owners are Department Heads and Project Managers. Risk Owners manages individual risks according to the mitigating strategies developed for those risks. Their responsibilities are to:

- Recommend a risk tolerance level for a risk through consultation of the risk's stakeholders.

- Develop and manage risk treatment plans to mitigate risk, specifically significant & critical risks.

- Monitor changes of risks and the implementation of treatment.

The communication of risk is essential to the success of the Corporation's governance of its risks. A *Risk Reporting Procedure* will be developed through the Manager of Corporate Initiatives and the Enterprise Risk Management Working Committee. The Risk Reporting procedure will be approved by the Enterprise Risk Governance Committee. (8)

The key difference between the approaches is the responsibilities of the CRO. At the federal level, it is a full-time position. In smaller organizations, it is most often divided between the department managers and the governance committee.

Once the administrative structure has been decided, the composition of the ERM working committee, or team must be decided. The team composition helps facilitate the successful implementation of ERM. Similar considerations will occur for the teams at the department or business unit level.

SELECTION OF THE TEAM
Unless the organization is under a mandate, the selection of an ERM implementation team is up to management. For U.S. federal agencies and departments OMB has mandated that specific individuals be members of the Risk Management Committee (RMC). The Federal Highway Administration (FHWA) in its mandate to state Departments of Transportation is equally specific and detailed. It not only suggests that individuals with specific transportation related skills be members, it suggests that a facilitator be employed. In the state of California,

the risk analysis teams for the various agencies and departments are generally composed entirely of management.

Because of diversity of team membership, some general guides based on experience are useful. First, team membership should be broad based. There is a tendency for management, as in the case of California, to believe that only they have the requisite skills to do risk assessment. However, front line employees deal with the risks regularly. In fact, they are often aware of developing risks before management. Consequently, the frontline employees who can contribute the most to the risk identification process, based on their technical knowledge, should be considered.

The team should consist of 5 to 7 individuals. If the team is too large it could become unmanageable or veer off course. Neither circumstance is conducive to the successful implementation of the EMR process or its ultimate success. It should be an odd number in case decisions need to be made. The odd number means that there will be a majority on any vote.

With respect to team member selection, the most important decision is who is to be the team leader. The team leader should be committed to ERM and be able to articulate the team's vision, mission, and decisions. Further, the team leader should be someone who is respected by both frontline employees and mid-level and upper management. The team leader is responsible for developing the implementation plan, and ensuring the team meets the implementation schedule. The team leader also presents the risks and mitigative actions to upper management and the risk management governance committee.

The FHWA suggests the use of a facilitator. The facilitator's job is to ensure that all members are contributing and assist the team leader.

A good facilitator can, along with the team leader, help the team stay on track. However, there is a caution. If the facilitator does not have a firm understanding of the expected outcome, the product could be less than useful.

The author had the opportunity to observe a nationally recognized facilitator at work. It was fun watching how effectively group members were engaged. However, instead of the pony the group was supposed to design, the result was the proverbial three humped six-legged camel. Even the best facilitator can forget the objective and get lost in the facilitation process.

IMPLEMENTATION PLAN

Either concurrent with the team selection, or shortly after an implementation, a work plan needs to be developed. Ideally, the team leader should be involved in the work plan development. This ensures that the team leader has a complete understanding of management's expectations for the team and the timeline goals.

There are several important considerations when developing the ERM implementation plan. First, who is going to be trained first. ERM is new to most governmental organizations. Further, public sector managers are still coming to terms with the need to manage risks on an organization wide basis and in a proactive manner. Consequently, training is going to be a key to the successful implementation of ERM.

RISK TRAINING APPROACHES

The author broached this subject in a follow up to the meeting with the Chief Administration Officer. There are three groups which need immediate training if starting at the corporate, as opposed to the department level. These are the governing body, the Risk Management

Governing Council and the Risk Management Team. The degree of ERM training is different for each group. The governing body needs a basic understanding of ERM and why it is important. The other two groups need more extensive training, with the Risk Management Team requiring the most extensive training.

If the ERM process is to start with a pilot in one department, then that department's management and risk management team need to be trained as well. As the pilot or strategic level ERM process is completed, it and the training is cascaded across the entire organization.

Ultimately, the objective should be to have the ERM training conducted in house. This requires a core of in-house individuals who are sufficiency trained and knowledgeable in ERM. However, because ERM is so new in the government sector, an outside consultant or training may be necessary. The CERMAcademy, for instance, provides such training. One of the training modules the CERMAcademy provides is a weeklong ERM certification. Upon completion of the course and passing the test, the individual is a Certified Enterprise Risk Manager®. Tailored classes presented on site are also available.

The author attended a four-hour introductory ERM class conducted by a major consulting firm. While the material was good, it was at times out of date and focused on the private sector. Further, all the public sector examples were from the federal level.

One needs to be cautious when selecting ERM training. ERM is so new in government, often the references are from either the private sector or out of date.

WHERE TO START

The second implementation issue is: At what level is the implementation process going to start? Are you going to start at the strategic level, do a pilot project at the department level, or implement ERM organization wide?

It is the author's belief that starting at the strategic level is best. Six reasons support this approach:

1. Governing body and key upper level management need to be trained and engaged in the process quickly.

2. Risks identified at the strategic level are the ones the governing body are most interested in and need to manage.

3. Strategic risks cut across organizational silos. Consequently, they are fewer in number. Having fewer risks to deal with initially, makes the implementation process easier. This increases the likelihood for successful ERM implementation.

4. The development of a strategic risk mitigation plan provides guidelines for department heads, as they identify operating unit risks and mitigation efforts. In short, with the strategic risk taken off the table, department heads can concentrate on the risk specific to their departments.

5. By focusing on the strategic risks, the number of individuals that need initial training and the associated costs are reduced.

6. This core group of ERM trained and risk assessment employees can act as trainers and aid the departments as ERM is cascaded throughout the organization.

While the author's preference has been stated, it needs to be noted that governments have used different implementation approaches. One such approach is presented below.

MOHAKARE SOUTH AFRICA ERM IMPLEMENTATION PLAN
Table 4 shows the work plan developed by Mohakare South Africa. In this case, Mohakare followed this sequence of steps:

Quarter	Activities	Key Performance Indicators
July– September- ber 2012	*Review Risk Management Policy and Framework *Review Fraud Prevention Plan *Conduct risk management workshop or all employees on Risk Management policy *Conduct risk assessment on macro-operations and pro-jects *Conduct operational risk as-sessment: -Income/revenue -Procurement -Reporting (Accounting) -Information and Technology -Municipal Planning *Include risk management in manager KPI *Develop risk registers and implementation plans includ-ing fraud risk assessment *Report monthly to manage-ment on progress made	*Approved Risk Manage-ment Strategy *Approved Fraud Preven-tion Plan *Percent Employees Trained *Risk Register: Macro-op-erational risks Risk Registers: -Income -Procurement -Expenditure -Reporting -IT -Municipal Planning *Performance plans for Managers and Direc-tors include Risk Manage-ment *Risk registers & implementation plans *Reports to management and council on the num-ber

	*Quarterly reports to Council, management and committee	of risks managed, not managed and in-progress

Table 4 - Management Framework and Policy Work Plan (9)

The Mohokare work plan includes a predetermined identification of the risk categories. In most cases, the identification of the risk categories is usually done during the risk identification process. However, as is shown here, management has a great deal of flexibility in determining how ISO 31000:2018 is to be implemented. It also has flexibility in determining the risk categories to be used.

SUMMARY

Even though ISO 31000:2018 does not mention the need for an implementation work plan, there are too many steps and too much risk information to be gathered, identified and assessed, not to have some time lines established for ERM implementation. Consequently, it is desirable to develop a work plan. The work plan describes the expectations, who is responsible for what and when activities are to be started and completed.

In order to implement the work plan, it is important to make certain decisions ahead of time. This includes the development of an ERM policy statement and risk appetite. In addition, an organizational implementation structure is needed. This structure includes the determination of the risk management committee members and the selection of the members of the risk identification committee.

ERM CHALLENGES

ERM should not be an isolated exercise, but instead, should be integrated into the management of the organization and eventually into its culture.

Focusing too much on internal controls. ERM includes internal controls but also larger issues of the external environment, as well as transparency, business practice, reporting and governance that helps define the overall risk culture. (Playbook)

It is important that the governing body and all levels of management be committed to ERM. If they are not, then it will be very difficult to create a positive supportive risk-oriented culture. Thus, the governing body must play an active and continuous role in supporting the ERM process. The involvement and commitment of management helps create an atmosphere which facilitates the implementation of ERM. The development of a risk management policy and risk appetite set the stage for ERM implementation.

KEY POINTS

- In establishing a risk culture in the organization, the following points need to be considered:

    o Governing body and management commitment to risk management is important.

    o Clearly stated ERM policy is important.

- Risk Management is continually stressed and made part of the decision-making process.

- Common and shared understanding of ERM and its relationship to achieving the organization's goals and objectives is present.

- Value and role of risk management in decision making is well understood and applied.

- Staff are encouraged to identify risks and inform management when new or existing risks need additional attention.

- Having an ERM development work plan is important for ensuring all the steps are followed within a specified period. It also communicates managements intent with respect to ERM.

- Strong diversified team can efficiently and effectively identify the risks, prioritize them and develop mitigative actions.

CHAPTER 5:
ISO 31000:2018 OVERVIEW

INTRODUTION

This chapter provides a general overview of the ISO 31000:2018. ISO 31000:2018 provides a standardized methodology for managing an organization's risks.

The use of an internationally recognized methodology provides the organization with two substantive benefits. The first is to provide a standardized approach which allows the organization to assess the risks it faces on an enterprise wide basis. Such an approach provides consistency and helps ensure all the participants assess the risks in a similar manner. The second benefit is it provides management additional support for implementing ERM. The use of an international standard shows that the ERM approach management is using is one used by governments around the world.

MINIMUM ERM REQUIREMENTS

The Federal Highway Administration (FHWA) in a report to state Departments of Transportation discusses the benefits of ERM.

> "As opposed to muddling through challenges, agency risk management provides guidance, tools and strategies that

help to anticipate these challenges and proactively address them." (1)

The FHWA also indicates that risk management is a new 'minimum requirement' for state transportation managers. However, the financial pressure governments around the world are experiencing, combined with the increasing intensity and frequency of natural disasters and other risks, indicate a comprehensive proactive approach to risk management is needed, if a perpetual cycle of increasing damage, repair costs and service reduction is to be prevented. In short, risk management is not a minimum competency for transportation managers alone. It is becoming a minimum competency for all public sector managers.

Before getting into the overview, there are two items which are worth stressing again. First, COSO ERM and ISO 31000:2018 have moved closer. In fact, in practice, elements of both models appear. For instance, while local governments in South Africa are required to use COSO ERM, references to ISO 31000 are appearing in their risk management framework. Similarly, the ERM approach adopted by the states of California and Washington are based COSO ERM. However, references to ISO 31000 also appear in their risk related documents.

The second point is that while the steps are sequenced, risk identification, analysis and treatment may occur at the same time. For example, during the discussion with the CAO it was mentioned that the city's fleet and maintenance facilities are under a major bridge. The bridge could be subject to earthquake damage. Should that occur some or all the fleet and the maintenance facilities could be destroyed, or response delayed due to debris blocking the road. This would hinder response. A slow response would be bad for the city's reputation and could cost lives.

While the probability of an earthquake is low, the consequences are high – damage to the fleet and repair facilities, lack of vehicles to respond and slow response due to debris. A failure to respond quickly adversely impacts the city's reputation and could cost lives. The risk treatment is to disperse the fleet to other locations.

All of this is commonsensical. While additional work will be needed to finalize the scoring and prioritization, going through all the steps in sequence may not be necessary.

ERM IMPLEMENTATION OVERVIEW

Since the ISO 31000:2018 steps are discussed in detail in successive chapters, only a brief highlight is provided below. The highlight should provide an overview.

The eight ISO 31000:2018 implementation steps are: 1. Scope, Context and Criteria, 2 Risk Identification, 3. Risk Analysis, 4. Risk Evaluation, 5. Risk Treatment, 6. Recording and Reporting, 7. Monitoring and Review and 8. Communication and Consulting.

Figure 2 below shows the sequence of the ISO 31000:2018 process.

Because the ERM process is continual, modifications to the risks will also be continually. This is shown in the Consult and Monitor and Review sides of Figure 2.

SCOPE, CONTEXT, CRITERIA
This step establishes the parameters for the risk identification process. By establishing the parameters, the organization ensures that the risks and mitigative efforts are specifically tailored to the organization. This in turn means that the resources spent on the mitigation efforts are implemented effectively.

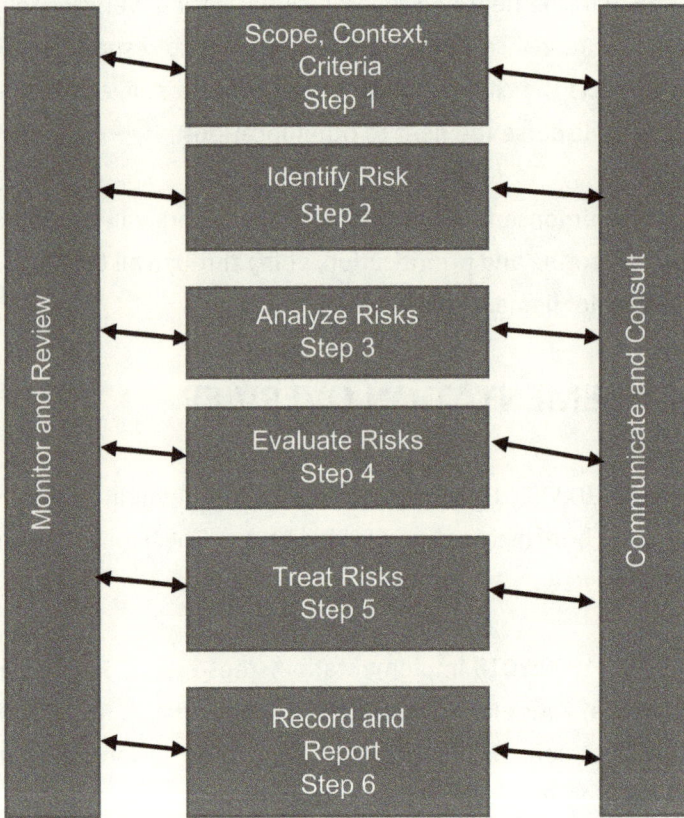

Figure 2 - ISO 31000:2018 Process

IDENTIFY RISKS

This step, when combined with the scope and context, leads to the identification of the more critical risks. For instance, if the local government is subject to hurricanes and not wildfires, then wildfire associated risks can be dropped from considerations. The purpose of this step is to identify all the risks the organization is likely to experience.

RISK ANALYSIS

This is where the risks are quantified. As noted in Chapter 2, ISO 31000:2018 takes an objective based approach to risk analysis. Thus, each identified risk is evaluated based on the probability of occurrence and likely impact. This analysis allows the risks to be prioritized based on the combined probability and impact score.

EVALUATE RISKS

Once the risks have been analyzed (scored), they need to be evaluated based on the risk appetite. The risk appetite reveals the risk tolerance. Those risks where there is little, or no tolerance require considerable mitigative efforts. Those with high tolerance, require less mitigative effort. In some cases, the organization will accept the adverse risk. In such a circumstance, no additional action is required.

TREAT RISKS

In this step, the mitigative efforts are determined. The extent of the mitigative efforts is determined by the risk appetite. The development of the mitigative efforts is the second to the last step in the development of the risk register. The risk register is the list of prioritized risk with the associated mitigative actions to be taken.

RECORD AND REPORT

The last step in the development of the risk register is to assign responsibility for implementing and monitoring the mitigative efforts. Also included in this step is the decision when to report and to whom to report the mitigative efforts.

MONITOR AND REVIEW

The last formal step is to monitor and review the risks and the associated mitigative efforts. This is a continuous process. New risks may be identified, assessed, treated and added to the risk register. Existing risks may be dropped. Similarly, mitigative efforts will be examined

> **ERM CHALLENGES**
>
> Hiring one individual to implement and monitor the ERM program for a mid to large size agency is problematic. Each agency should assess the level of support necessary to implement and manage ERM effectively. To be effective, the ERM program will need the appropriate team with knowledge and experience in risk management, leadership, and gravitas to build the ERM function. If an agency does not have a Chief Risk Officer or intend to hire one, it should also carefully consider where the core team fits in the agency to make it most effective. While agencies should be careful about building an ERM empire, the size of the ERM team should reflect the needs of the organization to support effective risk management. (Playbook 2015)

and modified as necessary.

COMMUNICATE AND CONSULT

The last ISO 31000:2018 step is to consult with management, the governing body and other relevant individuals to determine appropriate mitigative efforts and identify risks. The reality is that this step is continual and starts from day one of the ERM process.

SUMMARY

Increasingly, risk management is being considered a minimum competency for public sector managers. ISO 31000:2018 is an international standard which provides a comprehensive approach to identifying, evaluating and treating the risks an organization faces. Its use indicates management is taking a proactive approach to risk management. Because it is an international standard and comprehensive approach, it provides management protection against problems related to risk events.

KEY POINTS

- While the ERM process is sequenced, it is up to management to decide who is to be involved in the initial implementation process and when they must complete assignments.

- In the initial ERM development phase considerable work will be required to identify, prioritize, and decide how best to mitigate the risks.

- Once the risk management strategy has been developed, maintenance will require less time.

- Risk management is a new minimum competency for public sector managers.

CHAPTER 6:
SCOPE, CONTEXT, CRITERIA

INTRODUCTION

This chapter discusses the establishing of the boundaries and environment within which the organization operates. By establishing the environment, management ensures that risks are identified and the mitigation (treatment) efforts are specifically tailored for the organization. This tailoring ensures that the identified risks are those most appropriate for the organization. It also ensures the resources used in the mitigative efforts are efficiently used.

There are three elements to this step. These are: Scope, Context and Criteria. This chapter will discuss each element.

DEFINING SCOPE

The first step for the newly created risk management team is to place the organization within its environment and formally identify the scope of its activities. This is done by examining all documents which state the purpose of the organization and the processes that enables it to carry out its mission. In defining the context, both external and internal risks need to be identified. External risks include national or state rules or regulation that must be followed, natural hazards that are prevalent to the geographic region and outside political or social issues. Management has little control over the external aspects. Internal risks could include, personnel rules and regulations, organizational culture, skill shortages, budget limitations, and governing body policies. Management has considerable control over the internal risks.

An organization's scope is defined by its geographic, legal and operational reach. Scope would include developing risk related regulations and risk charter. Scope is also defined by its mission statement. An example of scope is the mission statement for the Marion County Housing Authority in Oregon. Its mission is to 'Provide Decent Safe and Sanitary Housing for Low and Moderate-Income People.' (The author was the Assistant Director of the Authority.)

The purpose, as defined by the mission statement, is to provide decent safe and sanitary housing. The scope is limited to housing for low and moderate-income people. Its charter is limited to areas in Marion County Oregon outside the city of Salem.

It is important to recognize that while scope identifies the limits to the organization's authority, risks often go beyond legal or organizational boundaries. Hurricane Harvey in 2017 for instance, impacted Texas, Louisiana, Mississippi, Tennessee and Kentucky. It flooded 800 water treatment plants, and 13 super fund sites. It spread sewage across the impacted area. It also wiped out roads and flooded public and private buildings. (1)

While defining the scope is important for determining the organizational limitations, understanding context is equally important.

IDENTIFYING CONTEXT

The context is the environment the organization operates in. It is derived from understanding its external and internal environment. It is an important aspect of the risk identification process because:

- Organizational factors can be a source of risk.

- Purpose and scope of the risk management process is interrelated with the objectives of the organization.

Those objectives are part of the context.

Continuing with the Marion County Housing Authority example, the Housing Authority had responsibility for all of Marion County outside the city of Salem Oregon. That is the geographic context. The staff dealt with county commissioners and their staff, as well as, the city managers and planning commissions of the cities in Marion County. Before new construction or acquisition could occur, approval from the planning commissions of the various entities and the city councils had to be obtained. That is the political context. Both are external aspects.

Because ERM is to be applied throughout the organization, goals and objective of each activity need to be identified and evaluated. The activities are generally identified as being strategic, operations and project management. The strategic goals, operational budgets and project specifications also provide context.

The Housing Authority's strategy would include the composition of new and existing housing, where to locate new housing projects and for what income level. This impacts decisions on which federal grants and loans to apply for and how to allocate resources both fiscal and human. Operationally, the annual budget and availability of staff provide constraints. Consequently, strategic goals were prioritized and factored into the operational plans. At the project level, the receipt of grants and loans allowed for new construction, acquisition or restoration of existing structures.

Another example is the decision by the Corvallis Oregon City Council to extend sewer and water to a site outside the city limits. The site had been selected by Hewlett Packard for a manufacturing plant. The City and Hewlett Packard negotiated a deal. The City agreed not to annex the site for five years and to extend sewer and water to the site. Hewlett Packard agreed to build the plant.

As incentives to obtain manufacturing plants go, this was small. However, when the next council election occurred, council members who supported the agreement were voted out of office.

Discussion with those voted out, indicates they felt the reason was opposition from Oregon State University, and the general feeling among citizens that immediate property tax relief was needed. The consequence of the vote was that city staff was limited on what it could do to attract new industry to Corvallis.

If one had gone 20 miles east to the City of Albany, this would not have been an issue. Albany, like Corvallis, has a city manager form of government. It is about the same size. However, it developed as a mill town. Albany wants economic development, since the timber industry in Oregon is declining and mill jobs are being lost. Corvallis on the other hand, because its largest employer is Oregon State University, is relatively insulated from economic cycles.

	Helpful	Harmful
Internal (within Organization)	**Strengths** What do we do well? What unique resources can we draw upon? What do others see as our strengths?	**Weakness** What could we improve? Where do we have resource concerns? (people, contract dollars, technology) What are others likely to see as weakness? What should we avoid?
External (outside the organization)	**Opportunities** What opportunities are open to us? How can we turn our strengths into opportunities? Or, can we create opportunities by eliminating weaknesses?	**Threats** What threats can harm us? What are our agency counterparts doing? What obstacles do we face? What threats do our weaknesses expose us to?

Table 5 - SWOT Analysis Concept (2)

Context identifies the unique characteristics of the environment the organization faces. In the case of Corvallis, the internal environment was established by both political decisions of the council and the relative insular nature of Corvallis from economic downturns, because of the location of Oregon State University.

SWOT ANALYSIS

One of the most frequently used approaches to the determination of Context is a Strengths, Weaknesses, Opportunities, and Threats (SWOT) analysis. A SWOT provides a comprehensive assessment of the organization's context and contributes to the risk identification process. The SWOT analysis is designed to provide a broad delineation of various aspects of the organization and its environment. The delineations can be facilitated by having team members answer some basic questions.

The U.S. Office for Benefits Administration developed questions for the SWOT analysis. These are shown in Table 5.

These questions are important and have practical applications. Using the Marion County Housing Authority as an example, let's place context in an actual situation.

MARION COUNTY HOUSING AUTHORITY: A CASE STUDY

An opportunity occurred when residents of an unincorporated area of Marion County, called Labish Village, approached the authority with a desire to improve their community. The improvements desired included water and sewer system improvements, the paving of a street, park improvements and the construction of new single-family homes.

This type of project is usual for Housing Authorities, which are normally involved in the acquisition and construction of single and multiple family houses. However, the author and the Executive Director came out of city government, where such projects are normal. There were risks since developing a viable community improvement plan meant the plan had to be approved by federal funding agencies, the Housing Authority's Board of Commissioners, the Marion County Commissioners and County Community Development, Engineering and Parks Department staff. Failure to obtain the approvals would doom the project. Such a failure would also damage the authority's reputation.

The Authority was successful in obtaining the needed approval and implementing the improvement project. It was also successful in completing a federal grant which was ranked number 8 on the funding list. The grant would have expanded the improvement efforts. In the first round of grant funding the first six were selected. A second round was scheduled for six months later.

The Labish project was pretty much assured of funding in the second round. It would have been funded, except there was a change in administration at the federal level. The new administration cut funding for housing and redevelopment grants. The second round of funding was cancelled. Continuation of the Labish Village project ended.

A weakness of the Authority was its dependence on federal housing funds. A threat was that the funds would be cut. This is what happened. Because federal housing money was reduced, the Housing Authority was forced to concentrate on maintaining its existing units.

With this background a SWOT can be developed for the Marion County Housing Authority. Such a SWOT is presented in Table 6.

STRENGTHS	WEAKNESSES
• High level of executive knowledge and engagement. • Governing body allows flexibility • Executives, management, and staff understand. challenges and design doable workarounds • Positions knowledgeable and experienced with project development	• Resources limited by federal funds. • Federal legislation restricts how federal funds spent • Must obtain prior approval from • local governments prior to implementation of projects. • Low income housing projects associated in public's mind with poorly maintained high rises that contribute to crime and drug problems.
OPPORTUNITIES	**THREATS**
• Develop Labish Village redevelopment plan • Work with multiple organizations to complete project, completion of project win for all involved. • Enhance positive reputation for Authority • Increase in federal funds.	• Not meeting organizational objectives. • Decrease or termination of funding. • Local government do not allow • project development. • Reduced funding does not allow Authority to maintain units adequately. • Inadequately maintained units • Negative public opinion of low-income housing.

Table 6 - SWOT MARION COUNTY HOUSING AUTHORITY

While this SWOT example is for a quasi-governmental agency, the same procedures can be used at a strategic, operational or project level for any government organization. The structural format will be the same. Further, the Labish Village example shows how an organization can take advantage of an opportunity, be successful in the completion of a project, yet have external events impact funding and resources. The adverse impact of such an event can require a substantive readjustment to operational activities and strategic focus. In the case of the Housing Authority, it was an adverse risk event, a reduction in federal funding. It could have easily been a natural disaster or a cyber-attack which required major unanticipated expenditures.

MOGALE CITY LOCAL MUNICIPALITY SOUTH AFRICA
The SWOT is an important tool for placing the organization's risk within its proper context. Table 7 shows a SWOT developed by the Mogale City Local Municipality of South Africa for their Strategic policy. While the weaknesses are to be developed later, the threats like Economic Recession, Inadequate Resources and Vandalism of the infrastructure are risks to the accomplishment of the city's mission. (3)

Opportunities are to develop alternative revenue sources and to strengthen the economy. This is exactly what the Chattanooga EPB did. Risk mitigation efforts provide an opportunity for organizations to find innovative solutions.

DETERMINING RISK CRITERIA
The third element in this step is determining the risk criteria. It is a carryover from the 31000:2009 version. ISO indicates the criteria are the objectives against which the risk is to be evaluated. They are the laws, mission statements, and objectives which affect the organization and determine the direction of its performance. ISO 31000:2018 lists elements that should be considered when determining risk criteria. These are:

STRENGTHS	WEAKNESSES
Business leadership / management Organisation culture (work ethic) Strategic positioning Stakeholder relations management / communication Business performance Management (systems, policies) **Resource management** Financial management Asset management Information / knowledge management	To be developed later
OPPORTUNITIES	**THREATS**
• Revenue generation alternative sources • ICT developments • Economic diversification Tourism opportunities o Job creation opportunities o International events o Mining charter o Agriculture	Non-payment culture in community and government department Inadequate resources to deal with increasing demands Economic recession Poverty / unemployment impacting negatively on available resources High electricity tariffs / penalties Electricity supply capacity Vandalism of infrastructure Gaps in legislation

Table 7 Mogale City Local Municipality South Africa

PRACTICAL TIPS

Make sure the context step is not missed. This step helps with the understanding of risk alignment, planning, and mitigation occur.

- How consequences (both positive and negative) and likelihood will be defined and measured.

- Time-related factors.

- Consistency in the use of measurements.

- How the level of risk is to be determined.

- How combinations and sequences of multiple risks will be considered.

- Organization's capacity.

The actual process for determining the risk criteria is not explained. As a practical matter the determination of aspects of the risk criteria should occur later in the process. This is because the determination of the likelihood and consequences and the combination of sequences are more appropriate at the risk evaluation step.

The organization's capacity, however, can be assessed as part of the SWOT process. This is because capacity incorporates human and financial resources, as well as, the organization's culture, history and reputation. All of which can be identified as contributing to a strength, weakness, opportunity or threat.

The state of Victoria Australia indicates that:

> **ERM CHALLENGES**
>
> Failure to adequately define the organization's context and scope of
>
> activities

> "Risk criteria define appetite for categories of risk. Risk criteria
> should be used in the decision-making process to develop a
> shared understanding about how much risk, the type of risk and
> amount of risk an agency wants to accept for its objectives, pro
> jects or initiatives.(4)

Under this approach the risk criteria are the risk appetite the governing body and management decide upon. But according to the elements listed by ISO it is the consequences and likelihood factors.

Most governments ignore this element.

SUMMARY

The first step in ISO 31000:2018 is to determine the Scope, Context and Risk Criteria. As noted, the risk criteria elements are not well defined, and most organizations ignore this element.

The scope is the legal, geographic and administrative boundaries the organization operates in. This can be determined from the organization's charter, mission statement, impacting regulations and laws and past practice.

The scope identifies the organization's limiting factors. These can be legal, geographic or monetary. These limits will ultimately impact the treatment options.

The context the organization operates in also impacts the treatment options. Recognizing the context determines whether an organization is subject to floods or wildfires. It is key to identifying the appropriate risk and what mitigative efforts are important. As noted in the Corvallis example, the city council vote impacted what city staff could do as far as recruitment of new industry.

Placing the risks within the organization's context, also assures that only those risk which are applicable are presented for treatment. This, in turn, provides confidence that resources are being expended on mitigative efforts in the most efficient manner.

An important technique used to determine the context and assist with risk identification is the SWOT analysis. SWOT identifies the Strengths, Weaknesses, Opportunities and Threats an organization faces.

Opportunities and strengths indicate areas the organization can use intelligent risk concept when dealing with risks. Weakness and threats indicate the limitation on mitigative actions and the associated risks.

KEY POINTS

- Scope determines the boundaries the organization operates in.

- Scope can be identified by examining the mission statement, charter and any other regulatory and legal impactful documents.

- Context identifies the environment the organization operates in.

- Context includes the geographic, economic, social and political environment.

- Placing the risks in the organization's context ensures that resources for risk mitigation are allocated in the most efficient manner.

- Strength, Weakness, Opportunities, and Threats (SWOT) analysis helps identify the organizations context and associated risks.

- Strength and opportunity help identify the area where the organization can be innovative.

- Threats are potential risks, while weaknesses point to the limitations to the mitigative efforts.

- Do not spend much time trying to figure out what risk criteria means. Instead, make sure risk appetite and the criteria used to score the results is well defined.

CHAPTER 7:
RISK IDENTIFICATION

INTRODUCTION

The risk identification committee has identified the organization's scope and context. It has conducted a SWOT analysis. The SWOT identified weaknesses and threats. Since these can be translated into risks it is time for the second step in the ISO 31000:2018 process: Risk Identification.

PURPOSE OF RISK IDENTIFICATION

The purpose of risk identification is to find, recognize and describe risks that might prevent an organization from achieving its objectives. There are four activities in this step:

1. Description of the risk. This allows the risk to be clearly communicated.

2. List the risks. This is the generation of as many risks as the team can think of.

3. Separate the risks according to whether they are primarily caused by a source external or internal to the organization.

4. Place the externally and internally identified risks into broad categories, such as: political, social, economic, reputation,

cyber security, etc. (It should be noted that, as in the case of the Mohokare work plan discussed in Chapter 3, the Governing body or senior management may decide on the risk categories ahead of time.)

As a result, the categories will have been established for the team. For the purposes of this presentation, the development of the risk categories is going to be the team's responsibility.

As noted earlier, ISO 31000:2018 approach is objective based. Consequently, risks are identified based on whether they will impact the organization's mission, goals, or objectives. Since ERM is more generally focused on preventing or reducing the adverse impact of the risk, the concentration is generally on those which have an adverse impact.

ISO 31000:2018 is designed to help preserve the organization's resources by proactively identifying risk and taking mitigative action. The mitigative action helps reduce the adverse impact of the risk. It thereby protects resources. A good risk description helps with this process.

DESCRIBE THE RISK

The State of Victoria Australia indicates that a "well-described risk is important to provide context and meaning of the cause, event, and impact for management and oversight. Key reasons are that it will:

- Help direct controls, assessments and treatment planning.

- Provide meaningful information for reporting and oversight.

- Reduce over or under investment in unnecessary treatment.

- Align the uncertainty to an objective(s)."(1)

Risk identification and their description may take several attempts and a lot of discussion. Below are some tips for describing risks.   It may be useful to test the risk description with someone who is not a risk owner.

1. **Develop meaningful risks:** When defining risks, agencies should consider risks that are most relevant to agency mission. Risk should not be limited to specific activities. Recognize that any single risk may be associated with more than one activity, section or department.

2. **Use common language:** Risks should be described using a common language that resonates within the organization and to citizens, and the governing body. Remove jargon whenever possible.

3. **Identify risks outside organizations control:** Identify the risks that are within and outside of the organization's direct control. This includes third parties, vendors, or contractors, that present a genuine risk to an agency's mission.

4. **Document risks:** It is important that the identified risks be documented. This information is used later in risk evaluation and treatment and development and communication of the risk management strategy.(2)

IMPORTANCE OF RISK DESCRIPTION

A good risk description is important for two reasons. First, by having a well-defined risk, risks of a similar nature can be grouped together. This shortens the development of the list of risks (risk register) and makes the treatment (mitigation) more effective. Second, the risks and the mitigation efforts need to be communicated to upper level management, the governing body and citizens. If the risks are not clearly defined, gaining acceptance for the ERM process could be hindered. Experience shows there are several challenges that arise in describing a risk.

- **Identify risks as broad statements.** Broad statements are less informative and difficult to manage at either an operational or strategic level. An example is a flood. It describes what it is broadly, but not what areas are affected. Without knowing the areas affected, it is difficult to assess adverse impact, let alone mitigate that impact.

- **Identify risks as a cause.** A cause contributes to a risk event. It is not the risk itself. Articulating risks in this manner hinders the effectiveness of monitoring and measurement activities. An example might be poor drainage. Poor drainage can contribute to mud slides, sink holes, or floods.

- **Identify risks as incidents.** Incidents are risks that have materialized. Treatment plans would be focused on managing the incident not preventing the incident from occurring again. An example might be flood damage at pump station #1. In this case, the damage is repaired, but the flood is treated as a one-time occurrence. No additional examination or mitigative actions might be taken, leaving the root cause untreated.

- **Identify risk as consequences.** Consequences may be measurable but cannot be managed effectively as they do not represent a specific 'risk event'. Examples might be a sprained wrist or damage to the organization's reputation. The wrist is sprained, and the reputation damaged, but what caused the risk to be sprained or the reputation to be damaged?

- **Identify a risk as a 'type' of risk.** For example, Occupational Health and Safety or Information Technology are types of risks. But Is the event a chemical explosion, which would be

Occupational Health and Safety related, or an accidental breach of information technology security by a careless employee? (3)

With the need to accurately describe the risk in mind, it is time to identify and list the risks.

LIST THE RISKS

A common group decision making techniques, used to identify risks is called Brain Storming.

Brainstorm
Brainstorming is a technique designed to generate as many ideas as possible. Each team member in succession identifies as many risks as he/she can think of. There is no concern for right or wrong, duplication or applicability at this point. The risks are simply identified and written down. Nor is the list of risks identified in the brain storming session the only risks to be used. As the group moves through the process, other risks may come to mind. As other risks are identified they should be added to the list.

An example of a basic risk list might be:

- Wildfires.

- Flooding.

- Legislation.

- Workforce eligible to retire.

- Lack of funding.

- Data security.

- Organization's reputation damaged.

Once the team has listed as many risks as it can think of, some winnowing down can start. In this example, there is wildfires. This is generally stated and conflicts with the risk definition process. Further, when the risks are examined considering the organization's context, wildfires seldom occur. Consequently, based on context, it can be dropped.

Flooding is equally general. However, team discussion determined there are two areas where flooding has occurred in the past. These are in Subdivision B and the area around Pump Station 4. These should be added. The general risk of flooding can be dropped.

Generalities like Legislation and Lack of Funding can be broken down further. In the United Kingdom, British Exit from the European Union is an important legislative consideration. It is often listed separately. Another example is the Oregon Legislature's passage of the Equal Pay Act. This act requires all state agencies, local governments and school districts to pay the same amount for men and woman who are doing comparable work. (It should be noted that the author was a member of the state's Comparable Worth Team when this was first implemented in the 1990s.

As such I was involved in conducting desk audits, developing job descriptions and scoring the jobs for placement into the classification system. To do this work correctly, regardless of the assessment protocol, takes time.) This legislation will divert staff time. Further, there is no compensation attached. It is, therefore, an unfunded mandate.

SIZE OF RISK LIST
During the discussion with the CAO, a concern was raised about the number of potential risks that can be developed as a result of the brain

storming. The concern was raised because the city of Edmonton Canada wished it had not started with 100 risks. I responded that I was not concerned with the number of risks for two reasons. First, it will be unusual for an organization, after filtering and prioritizing the risks, to have 100 risks of the highest priority. The second reason is that once the risk register is computerized, even 100 risks is easy to manage.

After the risks are listed, the next step is to identify which risks are external and internal.

EXTERNAL AND INTERNAL RISKS

The identification of which risks are external and internal in origin helps identify the most pertinent risk. Separating the risks as to whether they are external and internal helps categorize them. This in turn helps with their eventual prioritization. Some of the external risks are natural disasters, legislation, economic disruption, citizen action, unfunded mandates and cyber-attacks. Internal risks include fraud, revenue limitations, organizational culture, staff retention and staff capabilities. Knowing whether the cause is from an external or internal source also assists in determining the level of control the organization has over the risk. Management has a great deal of control over internal risks. Management does not have as much control over external risks. Knowing this helps shape the mitigation efforts. Using the external and internal filter and the risk definition the list of risk might look like that presented in Table 8.

Obviously, flooding and unfunded mandates are external to the organization. While ten percent of the workforce is eligible to retire, and the computer system needs to be upgraded are internal risks. A citizen's group is agitating against council policies, is an example of a risk that can negatively impacting the council's reputation. This risk could be external to the political environment the organization operates in, or internal to the organization's administrative boundaries.

	Risk
External	Flooding Subdivision B
	Flooding Pump Station 4 area
	Unfunded Mandate
	Citizen Group Agitating against policies – damage to reputation
Internal	Ten percent of workforce eligible to retire
	Computer system out of date needs to be updated.

Table 8 Example 1

This process of identifying the risks and placing them in the internal or external category is followed for all the identified risks. The narrowing and grouping are furthered in the next step. That step is the categorizing of the risks.

RISK CATEGORIES

A risk category identifies a 'type' of risk. This makes it easier to understand the context of the risk and develop a profile of risks. The risk categories form the basis for the risk register. The risk register is a key product of ERM. The goal is to develop a risk management strategy.

ISO 31000:2018 lists several risk categories. They are separated by their external and internal context. The external context includes: social, cultural, political, legal, regulation, financial regulatory, technological etc. The internal context includes: governance, organizational structure, policies, information systems, organization culture, etc. The categorizing of the risks is generally tailored to the organization.

> **PRACTICAL TIPS:**
>
> Each organization should decide what risk categories make sense for its context and operations.

WARWICK SHIRE COUNTY COUNCIL RISK CATEGORIES

The Warwick Shire County Council UK has developed a more extensive set of risk categories than ISO 31000:2018 recommends. Its risk categories are presented in Table 9. While some are the same as ISO 31000:2018, such as political, legal (regulatory), Warwick Shire includes opportunities, reputation, citizens and environment. Warwick Shire also indicates the types of risks which fall under each category.

Another approach to identifying what risk should go into what category is to define the category in a general way. An example for Operational and Reputational risk categories below.

OPERATIONAL RISK

Operational Risk is the potential loss attributable to process variation or disruption on operations caused by internal or external factors. Unlike strategic risks, which can impact the entire organization and its survival, the impact of Operational risk is limited. It generally affects a portion of the organization for a limited period.

REPUTATIONAL RISK

Reputational risk is the impact on the organization's reputation due to the risk event occurrence. The Warwick Shire lists negative publicity and increased complaints. Other adverse risks are failure to complete a project, fraud and corruption, mismanagement etc. Bad press can result in a loss of revenue, decline in morale and difficulty recruiting qualified individuals. An increase in legislative and regulatory scrutiny can also occur. A good reputation may facilitate passage of revenue measures, favorable legislation, an increase in morale and the ability to recruit highly qualified individuals

Political	<ul><li>Change in Government policy</li><li>Member support / approval</li><li>Political personalities</li><li>New political arrangements</li></ul>
Economic	<ul><li>Demographics</li><li>Economic downturn - prosperity of local businesses / local communities</li></ul>
Regulatorily	<ul><li>Legislation and internal policies/regulations including: Health & Safety at Work Act, Data Protection, Freedom of Information, Human Rights, Equalities Act 2010 and Employment Law.</li><li>Grant funding conditions</li><li>Legal challenges, legal powers, judicial reviews</li><li>Or Public interest reports</li></ul>
Finance	<ul><li>Budgetary pressures</li><li>Loss of/reduction in income/funding, increase in energy costs</li><li>Cost of living, interest rates, inflation etc.</li><li>Financial management arrangements</li><li>Investment decisions, Sustainable economic growth</li><li>Affordability models and financial checks</li><li>Inadequate insurance cover</li><li>System / procedure weaknesses that could lead to fraud</li></ul>
Opportunities/ Outcomes	<ul><li>Add value or improve customer experience/satisfaction</li><li>Reduce waste and inefficiency</li><li>Raising educational attainment and improving the lives of children, young people and families</li><li>Maximising independence for</li></ul>

	older people with disabilities
	• Developing sustainable places and communities
	• Protecting the community and making Warwickshire a safer place to live
Reputation	• Negative publicity (local and national), increase in complaints
Management	• Loss of key staff, recruitment and retention issues
	• Training issues lack of/or inadequate management support
	• Poor communication/consultation
	• Capacity issues - availability, sickness absence
	• Emergency preparedness / Business continuity
Assets	• Property - land, buildings and equipment,
	• Information – security, retention, timeliness, accuracy, intellectual property rights
	• ICT – integrity, security, availability, e-government
	• Environmental - landscape, countryside, historic environment, open space
New Partnerships/ Projects/ Contracts	• New initiatives, new ways of working, new policies and procedures
	• New relationships – accountability issues / unclear roles and responsibilities
	• Monitoring arrangements
	• Managing change
Customers	• Changing needs and expectations

/ Citizens	of customers • Poor communication/consultation • Poor quality / reduced service delivery - impact on vulnerable groups • Crime and disorder, health inequalities, safeguarding issues
Environment	• Recycling, green issues, energy efficiency, land • Use and green belt issues, noise, contamination, pollution, increased waste or emissions, • Impact of planning or transportation policies • Climate change – hotter drier summers, milder wetter winters and more extreme events – heat waves, flooding, storms etc

Table 9 - Risk Categories Warwick Shire County Council UK (4)

In the ISO 31000:2018 categories, a computer failure is placed in Information Systems. In Warwick Shire, it would probably fall under Assets, which lists ICT availability. Mohokare places IT under operations. As noted earlier, a risk can fall in more than one category.

Similarly, as risks are identified and categorized, it will be found that several risks cross organization and activity boundaries. Identifying these risks allows management to consolidate them and devise unified mitigative actions, as opposed to having each department or agency develop their own mitigative actions.

EXAMPLE
Continuing with the basic risk example, when placed in the categories they would look like Table 10.

Risk Category	Risk
External	
Subdivision B	Flooding
Pumping Station 4 area	Flooding
Financial/Legal	Unfunded mandate
Political/Reputation	Citizen group agitating against council policies
Internal	
Operational	Ten percent of workforce Eligible to retire.
IT Computer	System out of date needs Updating.

Table 10 - Example 2

For each risk, a similar process of describing, identifying context and the placing it in the appropriate risk category is used.

FLORIDA DEPARTMENT OF TRANSPORTATION (FDOT) – CASE STUDY (5)

The FDOT was an early ERM adopter. It implemented ERM in 2015. In examining the short falls between existing FDOT practices and ERM requirements, it was determined that Project level risk management strategies were well established and very strong in the department, while enterprise wide or programmatic risks were not as well understood.

- Moving Ahead for Progress in the 21st Century Transportation Act (MAP 21) requires state Departments of Transportation to develop a Transportation Asset Management Plan (TAMP).

- TAMP is to include a Risk Based Asset Management Plan

(RBAMP).

- The two plans must be certified by the Federal Highway Administration (FHWA) by June 30, 2019. Certification failure will result in National Highway Performance Program funds being reduced by thirty-five percent.

FDOT identified twenty-six department level risks. Below are three of the identified risks.

- **External Risk:** State and Federal funding are significantly reduced across the board for transportation.

- **External Risk:** Sinkholes emerge under or near roadway sections compromising foundations. Sinkholes, either naturally occurring or due to infrastructure issues (water pipe seepage), compromise pavement integrity and are potentially catastrophic events.

- **Internal Risk:** The department's ability to efficiently deliver programs is undermined due to diversion of funds to high-profile projects.

Federal and State funding issues and the shifting of monies to higher profile needs is like risks faced by governments around the world. Sinkholes, as noted in Chapter 1, can cause substantive damage. This damage can cost a considerable amount to repair. The repair cost could require a substantive shift in available funds.

(To add some continuity, the above FDOT risks will appear in other chapters. The use of this example follows the risk process for a state level department.)

ERM Challenges

Failure to adequately describe the risks.

To return to the discussion with the CAO. If the risk identification team's mission is strategic risk development, the focus will be on those risks which management and the governing body deem the most important. These are risks that could have a significant adverse impact on the accomplishment of the organization's critical mission. The risks deemed not strategic can be passed along to the appropriate risk identification team. Generally, strategic risks are going to be those which have higher adverse impact scores or cut across organizational silos.

Once the risks have been separated, the risks are ready to be analyzed.

SUMMARY

ISO 31000:2018's step 2 is where the ERM process begins. Up to this point the risk appetite has been decided upon by upper level management. The team has placed the organization in the proper context and conduced a SWOT analysis. The SWOT analysis helps identify the organization's weaknesses and threats. These are areas which provide the team with the start of the list of risks.

Using the brainstorming technique, the team can begin identifying the risks the organization faces. The team states a risk and writes it down. Once the team has written down as many risks as possible, the team determines which risk is external or internal. After identifying the risks as being external or internal, the risks are be placed in a risk category. The determination of the risk categories can be done by either upper level management or the risk management team. There is flexibility as to the risk categories to be used.

Just as the allocation of risks to the external and internal categories will assist with the treatment strategies, the allocation of risks to categories assists with the development of strategies to treat the risks. For instance, when a series of risks are placed in one category, such as Unfunded Mandates, management can see all the Unfunded Mandates. This will help determine whether they should be dealt with individually or collectively.

In some cases, the risks can be dealt with by using a few mitigative actions. Similarly, the grouping may identify risks which cut across organizational silos. These may end up in the organization's strategic risk register, as opposed to, the operational risk register.

KEY POINTS

- Management has flexibility in the risk categories it decides to use. However, because of its importance, always include a Reputational Risk Category.

- Using the brainstorming technique, the risk identification team lists as many risks as possible.

- Identified risks are then categorized according to whether they are external or internal.

- External risks are those which come from outside the organization.

- Internal risks are those which are internal to the organization.

- Risk categories are the broad categories into which an

organization's risks can be placed.

- Management has considerable flexibility in determining both when in the ERM process the categories will be articulated and what categories will be used.

- There is frequently a concern that the number of identified risks will be too great for management to address. Computerization of risks facilitates risk management.

- Use of internal and external and the categorization of risks allows the number of risks to be reduced.

CHAPTER 8:
RISK ANALYSIS

INTRODUCTION

Risk analysis involves a detailed consideration of uncertainties, risk sources, consequences, and likelihood. A risk event can have multiple causes and consequences. Understanding how the organization's goals and objectives are affected by the event is an important part of the analysis. This chapter discusses the risk analysis step.

RISK FACTORS

Risk analysis can be quick and dirty, or detailed and complex depending on the time frame, purpose of the analysis and the amount of information available. ISO 31000:2018 recommends that the following factors be considered in risk analysis:

- Likelihood of events and consequences.

- Nature and magnitude of consequences.

- Complexity and connectivity.

- Time-related factors and volatility.

- Pace of change.

- Effectiveness of existing controls.

- Sensitivity and confidence levels.

The likelihood of the event and the magnitude of the consequence make it clear that an objective based approach is to be used.

Risk Analysis is necessary because resources are limited, and management wants to be assured they are using the most efficient process possible. There are numerous ways to analyze a risk. Some of the risk analysis techniques are quantitative. Sophisticated probabilistic risk assessment models are being developed for use in critical infrastructure, such as nuclear power plants. Other risk analysis techniques are qualitative.

The most common approach is the heat map. The heat map is used to score the risks based on the value given on a likelihood scale and an impact scale. It is easy to use. The heat map provides a nice visual. Most people can understand how the heat map works. Thus, it is easy to explain to citizens, stakeholders, and employees.

HEAT MAPS

A heat map is a graphic representation of the severity of an event into which the risk is placed. Figure 3 shows a five-gradient heat map. In this case, Consequences are rated 1 to 5, while Likelihood is ranked A to E. In most case, both sides are ranked numerically. The total score of a gradient can be additive or multiplicative. In a five gradient heat map using a multiplicative approach, a score of 25 score, means high likelihood and high consequences are each rated a 5. Such a score would place the risk in the upper right corner. It would be high on the priority ranking.

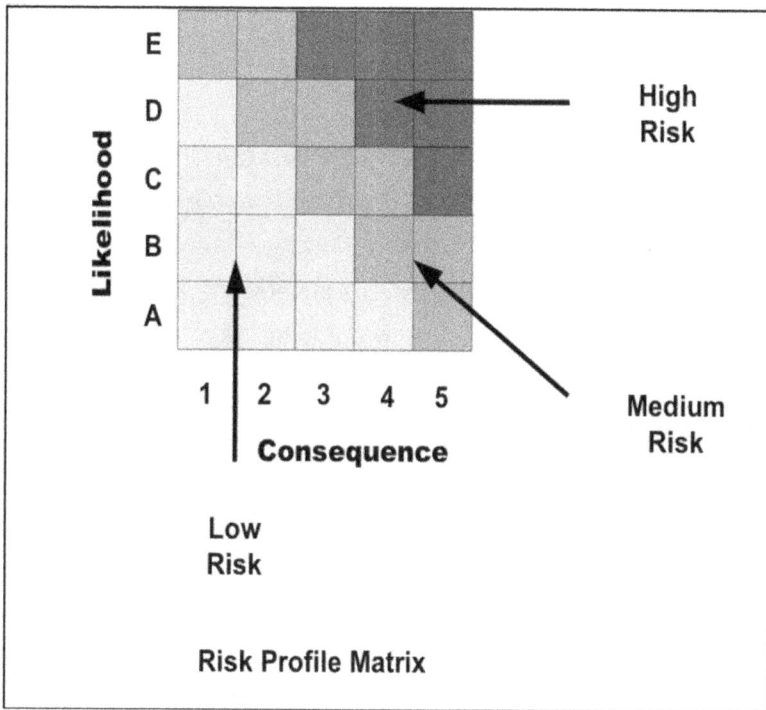

Figure 3 - Heat Map

Thus, when it came to decide on mitigative actions, a risk with such a score would be given substantive mitigative attention. A score of 1 would place it in the lower left corner. Such a score would be low on the priority ranking. Its adverse impact is deemed small. Unless there are enough resources to warrant mitigative action, its adverse impact would be accepted. No mitigative action would be taken.

While scoring the risk using a heat map may seem easy, it takes effort to be relatively accurate. It may require analysis of historical risk occurrences and their severity, as well as, discussion with other municipalities, technical experts on staff and perhaps outside consultants to determine a reasonable score. The objective is not to have a perfect score, because, in the continual monitoring and evaluation step, scores may end up being modified. The objective is to have a rating which is relatively objective and can be defended.

In Figure 3, the risks that are scored in the dark gray (high risk)) spaces would warrant mitigative action. Those in light gray (medium) might require some treatment.   The risk in the white (low risk) would have to be examined, but in most cases, the adverse impact would be accepted. Little or no mitigative action would be taken.

MEASURES USED IN THE HEAT MAP

It should be noted that the number of gradients used is determined by management. Some governments use a three gradient heat map. Others use four or five gradients.

Tables 11 and 12 show the Consequence and Likelihood Rating used by the Vale of Glamorgan Council in Wales UK. (1)

VALE OF GLAMORGAN COUNCIL CONSEQUENCE AND LIKELIHOOD RATINGS

In this case, a four gradient heat map is being used. At the extreme end of the consequence scale is a total shut down of services or a financial cost of more than £500,000. It is designated Catastrophic. The council has gone further in that the consequence is broken down to type of impact or risks. Thus, under Reputation, at the catastrophic level, Intervention by external regulators would be occurring. The detailing of the consequence for each consequence category provides considerable assistance to the team in assigning the risk the appropriate score, or category placement.

TYPE OF IMPACT	MAGNITUDE			
	Low	Medium	High	Catastrophic
Financial	Less than £50,000	£50,000 - £250,000	£250,000 - £500,000	More than £500,000
Public Wellbeing	Minor disruption to service for small number of people	Short term service failure having minor effect on public well being	Large scale service failure without effect on well-being or small-scale failure having significant effect on individuals	Total shutdown of service having detrimental effect on well being
Environmental and Social	No lasting detrimental effect on the environment and community	Short term local detrimental effect	Long term detrimental environmental or social impact	Extensive detrimental long-term impacts
Reputation	Increase in complaints	Local press coverage	National press & complaints upheld	Intervention by external regulators
Health & Safety	Minor injury	Minor injury to several or more people	Serious injuries resulting in hospitalization	Fatality

Table 11 - Consequence Rating Vale of Glamorgan Council

Very unlikely	Less than 10% chance of occurring
Possible	Less than 50% chance of occurring
Probable	Greater than 50% chance of occurring
Almost Certain	90% chance of occurring

Table 12 - Likelihood Rating Vale of Glamorgan Council

The use of categories communicates well. However, it is better to also assign a numerical value to each category. This is useful in that once the initial score for the risk is obtained, it can be compared with the impact of mitigative action or with the score in the next review cycle. Thus, if a risk has a score of 16, and it is estimated that the mitigative actions will only mitigative ten percent of the adverse impact, the remaining score for the risk would be 14.4. After all other mitigative actions are taken, this risk can be revisited to see what else can be done to reduce the score, or the risk can be highlighted and monitored throughout the reporting period.

Table 13 continues the risk example and adding a score from a 5-point heat map using a multiplicity approach. The risk analysis, based on informed judgement, determined the total scores as follows.

Based on these scores, the risks can be prioritized. The two flooding areas and outdated computer systems fall within the black area. Those risks rated as twenty would be at the top of the list. Those rated 15 would be next and so forth. The prioritization sets the risks up for the next step Risk Evaluation.

Risk Category	Score	Risk
External		
Subdivision B	15	Flooding
Pump Station 4	20	Flooding
Financial/Legal	10	Unfunded federal Mandate
Political/Reputation	5	Citizen group agitating against policies
Internal		
Operational	9	Ten percent of workforce eligible to retire
IT	20	Computer system out of date needs to be updated.

Table 13 - Example 3

ARGYLL BUTE RISK REGISTER

Table 14 shows two of the 15 strategic risk in the city of Argyll Bute in Australia.

Bute's risk register contains 15 strategic risks. The city used a five-point scale. The risks are related to probability of occurrence and the impact. It was scored as 12, with a 3 likelihood and 4 impact.

Argyll Bute has identified two finance related risks. One, incoming revenue is either reduced or insufficient to fund Council objectives or require service reductions. This is what occurred with the Marion County Housing Authority. It demonstrates that many of the risks governments face are common and universal.

Risk	Risk Description	Examples Consequences	Gross Risk		
			Like	Impact	Score
Finance Income and Funding	A major reduction in income/funding as result of a reduction in grant funding, reduced collection of taxes or fees and charges. This may arise from global or local economic circumstances, government policy on public sector budget	Lack of income/funding to support Council objectives. Requirement to reduce service provision or budget allocations. Reduced income impact on performance levels.	3	4	12

Table 14 - Argyll Bute Risk Register (2)

Where Argyll Bute has identified 15 strategic risks. The Wychavon District Council in the United Kingdom lists 18 risks in its 2017 Strategic Risk Register. (3) As noted earlier, the number of strategic risks identified by most government is relatively small.

FLORIDA DEPARTMENT OF TRANSPORTATION (CONTINUED)

Florida Department of Transportation Risk Analysis – Case Study continued (4)

FDOT uses a five-point multiplicative heat map. It adds additional points for Other Considerations. The consequence score is the average of the four consequences. To differentiate between risks and highlight key issues of importance a bonus score (Other Considerations) is included with .2 points given for each consideration for a maximum of 1 point.

External Risk: State and Federal funding are significantly reduced across the board for transportation.

Likelihood 2

Consequence Score

Safety 3

Mobility 4

Asset Damage 3

Other Financial Impacts 4

(3+4+3+4)/4 = 3.5

Initial Risk: 3.5 (Consequence) x 2 (Likelihood) = 7

Other Considerations

Funding Yes .2

Insurance No 0

Regulatory Yes .2

Political Yes .2

Reputation Yes .2

Other Considerations: .2+0+.2+.2+.2 = 0.8

Total Risk: 7 (Initial Risk) + 0.8 (Considerations) = 7.8 ~ 8

External Risk: Sinkholes emerge under or near roadway sections compromising foundations. Sinkholes, either naturally occurring or due to infrastructure issues (water pipe seepage), compromise pavement integrity and are potentially catastrophic events.

Likelihood 3

Likelihood	3

Consequences Score

Safety	3
Mobility	3
Asset Damage	3
Other Financial Impacts	2

(3+3+3+2)/4=2.75

Initial Risk: 2.75 (Consequence) x 3 (Likelihood) = 8.25

Other Considerations

Funding	No	0
Insurance	No	0
Regulatory	No	0
Political	Yes	.2
Reputation	Yes	.2

Other Considerations: 0+0+0+.2+.2=0.4 round to

Total Risk: 8.25 (Initial Risk) + 0.4 (Considerations) = 8.65 ~ 9

It is important to note the different evaluation approaches used by Glamorgan, Argyll, and FDOF. While each is based on a heat map, the decision on what constitute the scoring differs. Glamorgan uses a four-point scale. Argyll used a five-point scale. FDOF uses a five-point scale. However, it adds up to one point based on the presence of other considerations.

ERM CHALLENGES

- Failure to provide enough information on consequence and likelihood for risks to be accurately analysed.
- Becoming too sophisticated in the scoring process which make it difficult to both explain and defend.

This shows the flexibility management has in the risk valuation process. It should also be pointed out that the valuation can be associated with a standard practice by using a basic heat map. Even FDOT, which has added to the likelihood and consequence score, limits the other consideration score to a total of one point. This ensures that the scoring is not too far from that resulting from standard practice. Ensuring a close or similar association to universal practice, facilitates explanation and protection from general criticism.

SUMMARY

The analysis step is where the risks are scored. Generally, the score is determined using a heat map. A heat map allows each risk to be assessed (scored) based on the likely impact and probability of occurrence.

Management must decide the scale to be used on the heat map and the definition of the impact and probability. The resulting rating allows the risks to be prioritized for the next phase.

KEY POINTS

- Each risk needs to evaluate using a consistent methodology.

- For most governments this methodology is achieved by using a heat map.

- Risks are scored based on the probability of occurrence and size of impact.

- Risks can be prioritized based on their score.

CHAPTER 9:
RISK EVALUATION

INTRODUCTION

In practice, risk evaluation and risk treatment can occur simultaneously. Further all the information from the prioritized risks, their treatment, and who is responsible for monitoring the treatment ends up in a document ISO 31000:2018 does not mention. That document is the risk register. It is a key product of the ERM process. This is because the risk register physically shows the organization's risk management strategy.

The development of the risk register starts at the risk identification stage and is finalized in the recording and reporting step. Since ISO 31000:2018 has a recording and reporting step, the risk register and its elements will be discussed in that step.

EVALUATION OPTIONS

Risk evaluation compares the risk's total scores against the organization's risk appetite. This comparison helps management decide what it intends to do with the risk. ISO 31000:2018 lists five options. These are:

1. Do nothing further.

2. Consider risk treatment options.

3. Undertake further analysis to better understand the risk.

4. Maintain existing controls.

5. Reconsider objectives.

DO NOTHING

To do nothing means management has decided to accept that risk's adverse impacts. Such risks generally fall in the lowest range of scoring. They would probably have a total score from one to three, with those risks with a 4-receiving treatment if resources are available.

FURTHER ANALYSIS

An organization would undertake further analysis and reconsider objectives when management needs to make the decision on how to handle a risk with multiple implications or just needs additional information. Risks requiring additional study might also include risks where the proposed mitigation efforts might have negligible impact. The additional study would allow for the development of better mitigative efforts.

MAINTAIN EXISTING CONTROLS

Maintain existing controls assumes that some control has already been established. Such risk controls might be those designed to prevent fraud and embezzlement or to ensure cyber security. These are risks that are widely recognized and professional guidelines or practices have been initiated to deal with these risks.

Because risk evaluation is a continual process, mitigative efforts and scores might change based on new knowledge. The change in score would warrant a reevaluation of the treatment. In this case, management may decide that the existing treatment is fine, no further action

is required. On the other hand, new guidelines or additional information might warrant additions or changes to existing controls.

Reconsider Objective

Since the purpose of ISO 31000:2018 is to mitigate the risk which
might adversely impact the accomplishment of the organization's objectives, the risks are evaluated against the potential adverse impact
of the organization's mission or objectives. There may be times when
the risks associated with the objective are so great that dropping or
changing the objective is the better way to proceed. For example, the
original objective might be to reduce the flooding around Pump Station 4 through construction of a major drainage project. However,
grant funds may not be available to complete a large project. Consequently, a change in objective might be necessary.

IN PRACTICE MOST RISK WILL BE TREATED – EXAMPLE 4

In practice, most of the risks that government faces are going to have
to be treated in one way or the other. Turning back to the basic risk
example, Table 15, assume that as part of the risk appetite the governing body and senior management decided that reputational risks
will be handled at the highest level in the organization. In addition,
risks with a score above 15 should be mitigated in whole or part, as
are any risk having an adverse financial impact. For any risk with a
score of four or less, limited or no mitigative action is to be taken.
Other mitigative action will be taken should resources be available.
That decision will be handled at the department level.

Under these conditions, the flooding, citizen group risk and computer
system would be handled by management and the governing body.
The rest would be handled by the relevant department. The unfunded
federal mandate, since it is not likely to impact the entire organization's activities, would be handled by the appropriate department. In

Risk Category	Risk	Score	Treat
External			
Subdivision B	Flooding	15	Yes
Pump Station 4	Flooding	20	Yes
Financial/Legal	Unfunded federal mandate	10	Yes
Political/Reputation	Citizen group agitating against policies	5	Possibly
Internal			
Operational	Ten percent of workforce eligible for retirement	9	Possibly
IT	Computer system obsolesce/ Cyber-security	20	Yes

Table 15 - Example 4

terms of what is to be mitigated, all except the citizen group and the workforce retirement, based on the organization's appetite, requires mitigative action. The risk evaluation for this example is shown below.

While the above example is more oriented toward city government, reputational risk due to citizen complaints, cyber security and un-funded mandates are ubiquitous risks every government around the world faces.

Once it is decided that a risk will be treated, management needs to determine who has responsibility for that risk.

THE CLARE & GILBERT VALLEYS COUNCIL RISK DECISION EVALUATION STRUCTURE

The Clare & Gilbert Valleys Council Australia has established a specific policy on what risks are to be treated and by whom. The policy is shown in Table 16. (1)

Extreme	Requires detailed response by the CEO and Management Team, with urgent action required immediately
High	Requires management attention and targeted action. Will be monitored within agreed timeframes
Moder-ate/ Low	Rated risks will be monitored within the relevant Department
ALL	Identified risks will be monitored at least annually

Table 16 - Clare & Gilbert Valleys Council Risk Decision Structure

Risks rated as extreme require detailed responses from the Chief Executive immediately. Risks rated as high level require management attention and targeted action. Moderate or low-level risks are to be handled by the relevant department. Once all risks are agreed upon, they are to be monitored at least annually.

SUMMARY

The Risk Evaluation phase emphasizes an aspect of the ERM process that appears on the right-hand side of Figure 1. That is Communication and Consultation. As shown in the Clare & Gilbert Valleys Council policy senior management's involvement in the ERM process is critical.

Upper level management and the governing body will want to review the prioritized risks. The identification of any risk which will not be treated will likely occur at this stage. Decisions about who in the organization is to have input into treatment options may also occur at this stage.

At this step, the organization's risk management strategy starts to be fleshed out. For the strategy to be effective, it must have the backing of senior management and the governing body. The best way to ensure that there are no major missteps along the way, is for continual communication and consultation to occur.

ERM CHALLENGES

A failure to communicate.

KEY POINTS

- Risk appetite, senior management involvement desires and all other relevant documents should be considered when evaluating each risk.

- Best way to ensure there are no missteps is to continually communicate and consult with stakeholders.

CHAPTER 10
RISK TREATMENT

INTRODUCTION

The purpose of the risk treatment step is to help identify and implement the options for addressing the risks. Risk treatment includes the following processes.

- Formulating and selecting risk treatment options.

- Planning and implementing risk treatment.

- Assessing the effectiveness of that treatment.

- Deciding whether the residual risk is acceptable.

- If not acceptable, taking further treatment.

TREATMENT OPTIONS

It is the formulating and selecting of risk treatment options which defines the risk management strategy for the organization. The type of treatments or risk mitigation action available to an organization include:

- Avoiding the risk by deciding not to start or continue with the activity that gives rise to the risk.

- Taking or increasing the risk to pursue an opportunity.

- Removing the risk source.

- Changing the likelihood.

- Changing the consequences.

- Sharing the risk (e.g. through contracts, buying insurance).

- Retaining the risk by informed decision.

AVOIDING RISK

Avoiding the risk is simply figuring out a way to eliminate the risk all together. The easiest way is to transfer the risk to another party. Initially contracting out the activity was a way of doing this. However, with the interconnectedness of the global economy, the risks associated with supply chains are increasing.

The reality for government is that It is hard to transfer or share the risk. This is because many of the government's assets, such as, roads, highways and treatment plants are physical and nontransferable. Similarly, many of its activities are established by law or regulation. Without changes in these laws or regulations, covered activities are going to be nontransferable.

TAKING OR INCREASING RISK IN PURSUIT OF OPPORTUNITY

As in the case of the Housing Authority taking on the Labish Village project, innovative approaches often mean an increase in risk. Governments are particularly vulnerable to the additional risks associated with innovative projects. This is because of the very public nature of their actions and the varied interest groups. Further, if there is a mistake, members of the public make their displeasure known.

The EPB of Chattanooga is an example of an organization which took the risk of fiber optic cable and high-speed Internet. To succeed with the high-speed Internet, EPB had to succeed against the cable companies in state court and the before the U.S. Federal Communication Commission. These were the risks. There were also risks associated with the installation of the fiber optic cables. The reward was improved performance, reduced costs and with the development of high-speed Internet, additional revenue.

REMOVING THE RISK SOURCE

There are several ways that a risk may be removed. One way is to eliminate the risk all together by not carrying out the activity which could cause the adverse impact. Automation is an approach commonly used to eliminate human error. This approach works for internal risks. This is because management has significant controls over these risks. External risks, such as cyber-attacks and natural disasters, management has little ability to remove the sources.

SHARING THE RISK

As with avoiding risk, governments have limited flexibility in sharing risks. Contracting activities out can mean sharing the risk. Joint ventures with other governments or the private sector, however, is the most common form of risk sharing.

RETAINING THE RISK

The easiest way is retaining the risk by making an informed decision. This is essentially deciding the adverse impact is acceptable or manageable.

While all the above options are available to a government, for the most part, management will be focusing on reducing the likelihood of the event and its consequences or impact.

REDUCE LIKELIHOOD

The most common way of reducing the likelihood is through training. For instance, NIST stresses that cyber security is everyone's business. It recommends that thorough continual training, reminders during discussions with employees and the stressing of existing policies, cyber security awareness is increased. This increased awareness will reduce some of the employee caused cyber security problems.

Another example is monitoring and simplifying. This is exemplified in the safety walk. The most common safety walk is the regular assessment for Occupational Safety and Health Administration compliance. However, some localities use a Gemba Safety Walk. Gemba is the Japanese term for workplace. The workplace is anywhere work is being done. It can be a machine shop, water purification plant or an office. The walks are conducted at irregular intervals. Unlike the compliance checks, where there is a massive check list, with each box checked as the inspection progresses, the Gemba walk focuses on a few specific issues.

Management decides ahead of time the specific issues. As management proceeds through the walk, when an activity on the list is being performed, management stops and engages the employee doing the task. Management asks what is being done and if it can be done better, safer and easier. The idea is to engage the employee and the work team. Management, through the walk, seeks employee assistance in reducing activities which create physical stress on the body, particularly the back and upper body, and in making the task less complicated by reducing the number of steps. By reducing the physical stress on the back and upper body, the probability of these types of workplace injuries happening is reduced. By simplifying process, the number of errors occurring during the process should be reduced. Complexity increases errors. Simplicity reduces them.

REDUCE CONSEQUENCES

To reduce the adverse impact means eliminating or reducing the damage that the risk event may cause. The most common way of doing this is to increase resilience. Increasing resilience is a goal of FEMA in the United States.

The OECD advocates this in its review of risk management policies entitled: 'Boosting Resilience through Innovative Risk Governance'.(1) It sets forth detailed policies to accomplish this goal in 'Recommendations of the Council on the Governance of Critical Risks'.

For the most part, the OECD recommendations are like those advocated by the National Institute of Building Sciences. Those are to implement building standards which are higher than the 2015 International Building Code and the International Residential Code. Other options include capital construction projects both major, like the EPB of Chattanooga's installation of fiber optics or localized like the Labish Village project. Once the decisions are made on how to treat the risks, decisions must be made about who is going to monitor the risk.

TREATING THE RISKS

It should be noted that while the risk management team still has responsibility for developing the mitigative activities and finalizing the risk register, the governing body, senior management, department heads and technical experts will develop the mitigative actions. Communication and consultation are the watch words for this risk treatment.

At this stage, most governments using ERM have identified the risks that have enough strategic or corporate impact. Further, if a policy like that of the Clare & Gilbert Valleys Council is in place, then the strategic risks will to be dealt with at the corporate level. This group will generally include reputational risk, the highest rated risks and those risks which most frequently cut across departmental boundaries. The remainder of the risks will generally be isolated to a specific department or project. They will be allocated accordingly.

Having allocated the risks, it is time for treatment to begin. Each risk may pose several options. The flooding at pump station 4 provides an example.

FLOOD PUMP STATION 4 AREA TREATMENT OPTIONS

The flooding is not limited to the specific location of pump station 4 but to the surrounding area. That area needs to be defined geographically to determine the extent of the area impacted. If it is an area with substantive residential and commercial development, a major flood abatement project may be required. If the area around pump station 4 is not developed, then the mitigative action might be focused on pump station 4's immediate vicinity.

In the latter case, mitigative action might include ensuring that there is an emergency alarm which notifies repair crews of a pump failure. Having a backup generator located close by, but out of the flood level. Or having several mobile pumps and generators with hoses which could act as a stop gap until the pump station is running again. Beside the mitigative treatments aimed specifically at Pump Station 4, some minor projects to divert some of the flood water might be considered. As for financing the mitigative actions, it could come from existing Sewer and Water Department revenues. Otherwise it might have to wait until the next budget cycle for inclusion in next year's budget expenditures.

If there is development around the pump station, the work directly related to the pump station could continue. However, further analysis might be required to better understand the extent of the risk and the best treatment options. Such analysis might be done in house, or by an outside consulting firm. These are choices management must make. The cost of the mitigative action goes into the annual budget. If the flood abatement project around pump station 4 is extensive, it may require support from a tax levy or federal grant. The question then becomes, what to include in any such levy or grant application. Should it include just funding for pump station 4 area flood abatement. Or, should it include multiple projects such as flood abatement for Subdivision B, and road repair.

The how, with what and when, treatment questions are all part of the risk management strategy. The strategy ultimately needs to be incorporated into the organization's overall strategic plan. Similarly, the funding needs to be incorporated into the city's annual budget and where appropriate in the capital improvement plan.

FLORIDA DOT RISK TREATMENT - CASE STUDY CONTINUED (2)

Continuing with the FDOT example. Below is the risk mitigation efforts identified for FDOT's strategic risks.

External Risk: State and Federal funding are significantly reduced across the board for transportation.

Mitigation:

1. Department will prioritize projects based on overall impacts to the transportation system. Projects risks critical to

achieving agency objectives and performance goals are eliminated first.

2. Department does project expected reductions in performance related to key agency objectives under funding constraints and convey results to lawmakers and/or the public.

External Risk: Sinkholes emerge under or near roadway sections can compromise foundations. Sinkholes, either naturally occurring or due to infrastructure issues (water pipe seepage), compromise pavement integrity and are potentially result in catastrophic events.

Mitigation

1. Artificial sinkholes are caused by sewer or water pipe leaks. The department manages these risks by developing additional information on the subsurface elements. Communities with subsurface water wastewater pipes can be encouraged to develop a robust inventory of subsurface infrastructure with respect to age, and conditions. Large diameter pipes beneath critical infrastructure may be monitored remotely, by camera. Major new pipes could feature fibre optics or other nano-sensing technology to alert the department of significant leaks or imminent structural failures.

Internal Risk: The department's ability to efficiently deliver programs is undermined due to diversion of funds to high-profile projects.

1. Department will forecast expected reductions in performance related to key agency objectives if funding is reallocated to high-profile projects and convey these results to lawmakers and/or the public.

2. Department will continue to develop conservative cost-affordable plans that tier programs and project by relative priority.

3. High-profile projects are candidates for Public-Private Partnerships/concessions. When appropriate, the department will consider alternative mechanisms and advise legislators on potential options for alternative funding.

In the case of Pump Station 4, management has options which are primarily constrained by time and money. In the case of FDOT, most of its options for dealing with a lack of funding and the diversions of funds, is mostly to analyze, prioritize, and report the consequences to lawmakers and the public.

In the case of manmade sink holes, FDOT is taking two different approaches. One is to encourage local governments to deal with leakage. The reduction of water leakage and non-revenue water loss is something local governments, under smart city projects, are attempting to accomplish.

Thus, FDOT with this mitigation effort, is encouraging local governments to do what they want to do. With respect to larger pipes, and the use of fiber optic cables and continual monitoring, there is both encouragement and the prospect of technical assistance and grants to implement mitigation projects.

The FDOT's Man Made Sink Hole Mitigation efforts, the link to local governments and FEMA's strategic mitigation efforts, demonstrate how ERM is being gradually spread to all levels of government.

RISK CONTROLS

Having decided on the risk treatment and placed them within the strategic and operational framework, it is time to establish some controls which allow the determination of the effectiveness of the treatment. Risk Control is an action that maintains and/or modifies risk. ISO indicates that risk controls include:

> "any process, policy, device, practice, or other conditions and/or actions which maintain and/or modify risk."

The word 'maintain' was added to ISO 31000:2018. Consequently, ISO intends risk controls to be part of the treatment step. Controls are the administrative procedures the organization uses to govern operations. The idea is that the existence of these controls mitigates risks.

The State of Victoria lists some common risk controls. They include:

- Legislation.

- Policies, procedures, guidance material.

- Qualifications.

- Credentialing.

- Training and required learning.

- Code of conduct.

- Audit, reviews, investigations.

The difficulty with this list and with the emphasis on controls at this step, is that it does not add much to the treatment step. To be sure training can assist in reducing the probability of a risk event. But the treatment would require specific training geared toward the risk. Qualifications for positions sets a base for technical proficiency, but that is no guarantee that a specific risk can be mitigated by that individual. Most frequently, the idea of controls is rigid performance guides and production specifications.

More specifically there are three common issues with risk controls. These are:

1. They deteriorate over time.

2. There is uncertainty with the assumptions when the controls were designed.

3. Environment in which the controls operate may change.

For controls to have much meaning they should be assessed as to how they can assist with the specific risk treatment. But as noted above, there are some caveats. Any control system, if not regularly updated, deteriorates. Anyone who has dealt with U.S. federal rules and regulations knows that many contain elements which were designed to deal with circumstances relevant 20 to 30 years ago, but not now.

At the Marion Housing Authority, the cooperation agreements with local governments needed to be signed before low and moderate-income projects could be constructed in their jurisdiction. However, the agreement was designed during the depression in the 1930's. Many of the conditions it was designed to prevent are almost irrelevant today.

Similarly, the VUCA environment creates uncertainty. The speed with which change is occurring in an information/technologically driven global economy is impactful. It causes substantive disruption. Thus, assumptions based on past behavior patterns quickly become invalid. Change and adaptation are required.

The argument is not whether risk controls are useful. They are. The argument is that controls are not the end all and be all. There is a tendency to indicate that controls can reduce risks all together.

Let me use an example of a risk that the governing body, management and the general public agree is a problem. That is the misappropriation of funds. A friend who was the General Manager of a Sanitary District, had employees embezzle money from his organization twice. Controls were in place the first time. They were strengthened after the first instance. But, it happened again.

Similarly, my first call, when I worked at the Oregon Department of Revenue Local Government Section, was from an employee of a school district. That individual felt that the district would be short of money at some point. Consequently, he put money into a personal savings account to be used when the district fell short of funds. The call was to confirm with me the validity of his actions. Since one of my roles was to ensure that the law and appropriate regulations were being followed, I had to tell him his actions were unlawful and inappropriate. He said he would give the money back and resign. Since I heard nothing further from the district, and was sure management was aware of the issue, I presumed he did what he said he would do. In both cases, controls and regulations were in place, but the risk, misappropriation of funds, still occurred.

The last action in the treatment step is to make sure that each risk is assigned a risk owner. This can be a specific individual, department, section or project. The risk owner has responsibility for monitoring and reporting on the effectiveness of the treatment of that risk.

PRACTICAL TIPS: RISK TREATMENT

- Allocate a risk owner.
- Assess what additional controls are required to modify the risk.
- Ensure additional controls are operating as intended before re-assessing.
- Consider additional treatment if current ones are not effective.
- Document the treatment plan and progress.

The tips indicate an organization should document the risk treatment and how effective it is. It should also assign a risk owner who continually monitors and reports on the mitigation efforts, making adjustments as necessary.

SUMMARY

The risk evaluation phase emphasizes decisions on which risks are to be treated and how. The treatments can include actions designed to reduce the probability, or the impacts of the risk. The degree of treatment will be determined by the organization's risk appetite

Risk evaluation also requires the aspect of the ERM process that appears on the right-hand side of Figure 1, Communication and Consultation. As shown in the Clare & Gilbert Valleys Council policy, senior management's involvement in the ERM process is critical.

Upper level management and the governing body will want to review the prioritized risks and the assigned treatments. The identification of any risk which will not be treated will likely occur at this stage. Decisions on who in the organization is to have input into treatment options may also occur at this stage.

ERM CHALLENGES

- Failure to take risk appetite into consideration.
- Failure to explore all mitigative options.
- Stuck on one approach.
- Failure to seek out ideas from other parts of organization when mitigation not effective.
- Failure to document sufficiently.
- Failure to communicate.

At this step, the organization's risk management strategy is fleshed out. For the strategy to be effective, it must have the backing of senior management and the governing body. The best way to ensure that there are no major missteps along the way, is for continual communication and consultation to occur.

KEY POINTS

- Risk treatment should be allocated to the appropriate level within the organization.

- It is important that the risk appetite be taken into consideration.

- Risk treatment plan and treatment progress should be documented.

- While ERM concentrates on the avoidance of adverse risk, the pursuit of opportunities has risks. It is important to recognize ERM does not preclude undertaking opportunities. In fact, both ISO 31000 and COSO ERM recognize and encourage risks associated with innovative activities.

CHAPTER 11:

RECORDING AND REPORTING

INTRODUCTION

Having reviewed the risk treatment step, it is time to discuss the Recording and Reporting step. At every step in the process, the risk information developed should have been written down. The document upon which all this information is written is called the risk register. The risk register communicates to employees, citizens and the governing body that critical risks have been identified and treated. It essentially presents the risk management strategy.

RISK REGISTER

The use of a formalized structure allows for comparisons from year to year. The formalized structure also facilitates computerization.

The finalized risk register usually contains twelve elements. The elements match up with the ISO 31000:2018 ERM steps. There is the risk category, the risk identification, likelihood, consequence and total score. Also included are the mitigative actions associated with each risk and the risk owner. These come from the Treatment step. In addition, the register includes a risk identification number for easy access from the digitized file.

A discussion of the risk trigger is also provided, along with a contingency plan. A contingency plan shows what management will do if the mitigation efforts fail resulting in unacceptable residual risk. Residual risk is the risk that is left after treatment. Having this information is helpful in several ways. First, it tells how effective the mitigation efforts are likely to be. Second, it helps identify risks which are going to be difficult to mitigate. Such risks may require additional examination or multiple short term or long term mitigative efforts. Finally, the collective assessment of the mitigation efforts based on the residual risks can provide an indication of the benefit to cost ratio of the ERM process.

RISK REGISTER ELEMENTS
The risk register elements are:

1. **Risk category** – where in the risk assessment does it get placed?

2. **Risk description** – what is the issue?

3. **Risk Identification** – How is it identified and tracked?

4. **Project Impact** – What is the impact of the risk?

5. **Likelihood** - What is the likelihood rating of the event?

6. **Consequences** – What is the impact and potential consequences?

7. **Risk Rank** – Where in the hierarchy of the risks does it rank?

8. **Risk Trigger** – What are the triggers that would require implementation of a contingency plan?

PRACTICAL TIPS FOR DESIGNING A RISK REGISTER

- Describe risks so that they are meaningful.
- Review risks regularly and archive risks that no longer require active treatment.
- Consider how many risks can reasonably be managed by each risk owner.
- Determine which risks are important.
- Manage access to maintain the integrity of the content.

---

9. **Prevention Plan – How is this risk going to be mitigated or dealt with?**

10. **Contingency Plan** – What is the plan if mitigation does not work?

11. **Risk Owner** – Who is responsible for managing and monitoring the risk?

12. **Re**si**dual Risk** – The amount of risk that remains after treatment has occurred.(1)

The elements in the above list represent an ideal type. In practice, most of the elements are used in risk registers. As with much of ERM in practice, governments adjust according to their needs and preferences.

RISK REGISTER SASKATOON CANADA

Table 17 shows part of a risk register developed by the city of Saskatoon Canada. The example is for outdated or unsupported software and/or hardware failure.

RISK RANKING	RISK SCORE				TARGET RISK RANKING
Medium		Likelihood	Impact	Score	TBD
	Inherent Risk	4.00	5.0	20.0	
	Residual Risk	3.5	TBD	TBD	

Risk No.	Risk Description	Strategic Goal
A&FS-6	Outdated or unsupported software and/or hardware Failure	Asset & Financial Sustainability
Risk Lead	Corporate Performance	
Risk Narrative	Some IT systems and hardware may be outdated resulting in inability to meet business needs	
Key Impacts	Vulnerability to security threats Failures/crashes; catastrophic data loss Data corruption, instability Increased downtime, lost productivity, inefficiencies Loss of flexibility, responsiveness Service disruptions	
Root Causes	Resource constraints Competing priorities Absence of IT strategy, governance model	

Outcomes of Managing the Risk	A modern information technology infrastructure that supports program areas in the achievement of business objectives
Current Activities	
Controls	
1	A full assessment of the IT infrastructure is in progress

Table 17 - Risk Register City of Saskatoon (2)

The overall risk rating is Medium, with a total risk score of 8.55. Corporate has overall responsibility for monitoring the mitigative efforts. Among the key impacts of the risk are security threats, failures/crashes, data loss, down time and lost productivity. Among the root causes of the risk are resource constraints, competing priorities and lack of an IT strategy and governance model. At this juncture, because the risk is viewed as medium, the city has opted to conduct a full assessment of the IT infrastructure.

Because Saskatoon is conducting a study, it has not indicated any mitigative impact. It just provides the inherent score. The residual risk score is to be decided (TBD). The residual risk is particularly useful. Residual risk is the risk score after treatment. To show its usefulness let us turn back to pump station 4.

EXAMPLE 5 PUMP STATION 4

It has been determined that in the current year the Sewer and Water fund has enough money to cover the cost for installing a backup generator, upgrading the alarm system and doing some minor water diversion work. That diversion and the backup generator will reduce

Risk Ranking	Risk Score				Target Risk Ranking
		Likelihood	Impact	Score	To Be
Medium					Determined
	Inherent Risk	4.0	5.0	20.0	
	Residual Risk	3.8	4.5	17.1	

Risk No.	Risk Description	Strategic Goal
A&FS-6	Flooding Pump Station #4 Area	Sewer and Water/Health Safety
Risk Lead	Sewer and Water Department	
Risk Narrative	External risk. Flood to area damages houses and businesses, creates economic damage, reduced efficiency of city services, damages equipment at pump station #4	
Key Impacts	Property damage Loss of income Loss of property value impacts city income Repair to roads necessary Cost of clean up Damage to equipment at pump station #4	
Root Causes	Resource constraints Competing priorities	
Outcomes of Managing the Risk	Flood damage reduced, city revenue and resources protected	

Current Activities	
Controls	
1	Upgrade alarm system
	Install backup generator above highest flood level
	Apply for federal grant
	As for construction levy approval

Table 18 - Example 5 - Risk Register Flooding Pump Station

the flood damage by eight and a half percent. The engineering department has developed a flood control plan for that area. A federal grant is available and will be applied for. The grant will cover twenty percent of the project cost. The remainder will be put on a construction levy going to the voters next year. Based on this information, a version of the risk register for the pump station would look like Table 18.

Under this scenario, the total residual risk would be 17.1. This is an estimated eight and a half percent improvement due to the risk mitigation efforts. This information is important for two reasons. First, it tells management that just doing some flood diversion work and preparing the pump station does not have enough overall mitigative effect. Therefore, addition efforts must be made. The residual number is a quick reference which tells management what is working and what is not.

The second reason it is useful is in communicating to the governing body and citizens that management takes risk management seriously. The risk register visually shows the governing body and citizens the risks the organization faces. The seriousness of the risk, the actions being taken to reduce their impact and the residual risk scores are also shown.

Risk Register Flow

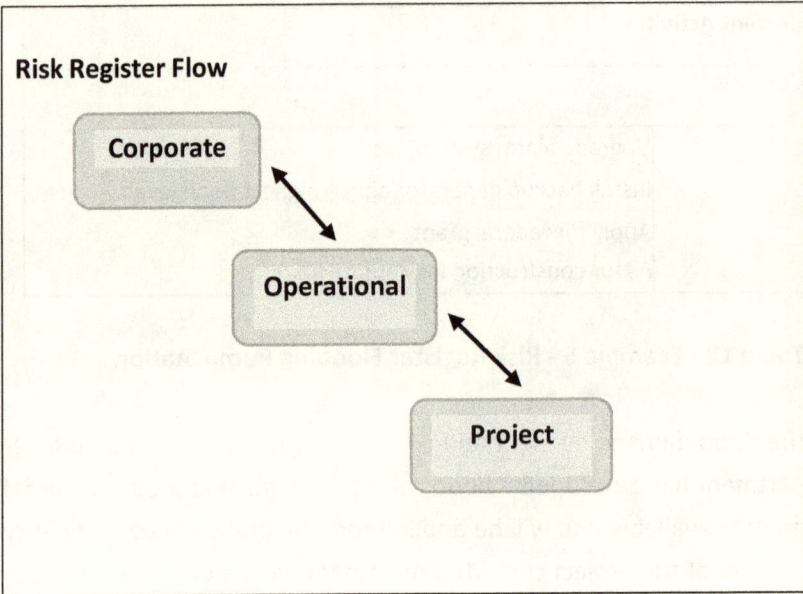

Figure 4

An important integrative question is: Is risk management integrated into existing governance and decision-making structures and performance- reporting systems?

RISK REGISTER FLOW

To answer this question, the results of the risk registers should be incorporated into the organizations planning process. Figure 4 shows flow of risk registers from one level to another. The Corporate Risk Registers will give due consideration to relevant partnership arrangements including community planning. Generally, Corporate risks are those risks that cut across organizational silo, have the highest total score and deemed by management and the governing body as those they want to deal with. The Operational risk registers includes the risks most appropriately handled by individual departments. Subsidiary risk registers should also be created and maintained at the individual project level.

> **ERM CHALLENGES**
>
> Failure to fully integrate the results of the ERM process into the organization's daily processes.

Examination of the organization's risk will show that many risks flow between levels. Identification of these risks allow them to be managed at the most appropriate level. This level of detail facilitates communications with employees about their responsibility in managing risks. It also helps communicating with the governing body and citizens.

SUMMARY

Once the risks have been identified and treatment options reviewed and identified, the results are recorded on the risk register. The register lists the risks in priority order and indicates who has responsibility for monitoring and reporting on the results of the mitigation efforts.

Generally, the governing body determines how often it wishes to have the risk management efforts reported. Similarly, management decides how often the information is to be reported to them.

KEY POINTS:

- Risk register should be developed and maintained by appropriate personnel.

- Risk register should list the most important risks according to priority, the mitigative actions and who is responsible for monitoring the risk.

CHAPTER 12:
MONITORING AND REVIEW

INTRODUCTION

Once the risk register has been finalized and the risk management strategy implemented, the next step in the ERM process begins. ISO has made this a twostep process. One is Monitoring and Review. The other is Communication and Consultation.

The purpose of Monitoring and Review step is to assure the quality and effectiveness of the ERM implementation and mitigative efforts.

RISK MONITORING AND REVIEW

Monitoring and Review includes reviewing and analyzing information on the identified risks and providing feedback to management and the governing body. Monitoring is generally done by the individual or group assigned to the risk. The risk register example in the previous chapter, (Tables 19 and 20) did not indicate a specific individual but did indicate GM Corporate and Sewer and Water Department, respectively. Whether a specific individual is identified in the risk register is up to management. However, the designation of responsibility to a

Report	Owner	Reported to	Timeframe
Annual Risk Management Report	Council Risk Manager	CMT and Finance & Audit Committee	Annual to 31st March
Annual Service Risk Management Report	Council Risk Manager / ORMF	Services and Service PDS	Annual to 31stMarch
Interim Risk Management Report	Council Risk Manager	CMT and Finance & Audit Committee	Annual to 30th September
Services Risk & Assurance Register	Services	Services & Council Risk Manager	Quarterly

Table 19 - City of Glasgow Risk Report and Monitor Requirements (1)

department, section or project is recommended. The results of monitoring and review should be incorporated throughout the organization's performance management, measurement and reporting activities. This process provides continual feedback to on existing and developing risks.

GLASGOW RISK REPORTING AND MONITORING

Table 20 shows the City of Glasgow Scotland risk reporting and monitoring requirements.

The Glasgow reporting requirement indicates that the risk manager annually reports to the Management Team and Audit Committee. The

CONTROLS/ EFFECTIVE- NESS	POLICIES/PRO- CESSES/BY-LAWS	PEOPLE	TECHNOLO- GIES
Very Effective	Documented formal policy and/or repeatable process available to, known to, And in use by, staff	Knowledge, skills and experience available internally	Right technology is in place with access controls (passwords) within automated systems used to capture relevant policy, program, service, project or initiative information
Somewhat Effective	Partially or not documented, little known or out-of-date policy and/or process	Some knowledge, skills and experience available internally with access to external help	Out-dated technology with partial access controls and some level of automated systems
Not Effective	No policy and/or process	No knowledge, skills and experience available internally	No or out-dated technology with no access controls

Table 20 - City of Oshawa Canada Risk Controls (2)

Annual Service Risk Management Report is made by the risk manager to the services. The services provide management an update on their progress quarterly. In this case, it is the Finance and Council and upper level management which gets the risk management report. It is expected that the Audit Committee report to the governing body.

While the reporting requirement does not include reporting on the plan to the public, the Audit Committee report is a public document which members of the public could access electronically.

In the case of Glasgow, a single individual is responsible for monitoring and reporting. This is a common practice once the risk management team has completed the risk register and the risk mitigation assignments have been made

An important aspect of the risk management report is an assessment of the effectiveness of the mitigative or risk control efforts. For each risk, the mitigative efforts and control effectiveness should be stated. The risk control effectiveness measures used by the City of Oshawa Canada are shown in Table 20.

Oshawa reviews three levels of control effectiveness. They are 1. Very Effective, 2. Somewhat Effective and 3. Not Effective. The city further indicates what those gradients mean for various risk controls. Thus, for People to be very effective, the appropriate knowledge, skills and experience must be available internally. Somewhat effective for Technology means there is outdated technology with partial access controls and some level of automated systems. Not effective for Policies or Procedures would be there are none.

It is in the monitoring and reviewing step that risk controls can be very useful. This is because controls contribute effectiveness. Let us assume, there are policies on how to operate a specific machine, yet several serious injuries have occurred to operators. Questions arise: Is the problem the procedures? Is the problem the training? Is the problem the configuration of the machine?

Any of these could be a contributor to the risk event - the injury. What the treatment owner, in conjunction with relevant management, would do is to determine the root cause of the accident and then assess the controls against the risk appetite. If the appetite is no tolerance for employee injuries, then the effectiveness of the control would be 'Not Effective' and modifications to the treatment would be made.

A risk control guide, like the residual risk score, provides management and the governing body with information on how well the mitigative efforts are working and where improvements need to be made. The presence of the control standards and residual risk scores, along with the integration of the ERM process into existing operations would allow the organization to answer: Does reporting on risk and risk management take place through existing management processes (e.g. performance reporting, ongoing monitoring, appraisals, internal auditing)?

RISK MODIFICATION

Because ERM is a continual process of review and improvement, risks can be added, moved or dropped. The Powys County Council for instance, changed the designation Corporate Risk Register to Strategic Risk Register. In the process of the original 28 corporate risks, 12 will remain in the Strategic Risk Register, 15 will be moved to the service (department) level and one will be dropped.

TRANSPORT FOR LONDON: CASE STUDY (3)

Transport for London (TfL) is the integrated transportation authority for the city of London England.

The initial approach to risk management was to emphasize the risks associated with financial health. Eventually, it was determined that the link between Operational, Program, Project and Strategic Risks needed to be better understood.

In 2015, it was determined that the seven strategic risks were diluting attention from real risks. As a result, the number of strategic risks were expanded to twenty-one.

In 2016, the Strategic Risks were reduced to 17. 'Non delivery of cost savings and efficiencies' was dropped due to changes to the Savings and Efficiencies Program. Other risks such as 'Planning projects without allocated funding', 'Increasing road congestion and deteriorating bus reliability and bus reliability' and 'Non-achievement of mayor's target for growth in cycling' were considered more operational moved to the appropriate department.

In response to the Audit and Assurance Committee an environment risk was split apart. The new risks were 'the TfL's Impact on the environment' and 'the External environmental impact on TfL.

Along with the adjustments to the strategic risks, mitigative actions change. These changes were in response to a safety report on a 2016 train derailment at Croydon. It found the driver was going too fast. The mitigative changes included:

- Chevron signs were installed at four sites with significant bends across the tram network.

- Lineside digital signage was installed to provide additional speed warnings.

- Options were being explored to transfer technology used on buses which monitor speeds and locations

- In-cab driver alert system was being examined.

- Upgrade to the CCTV system was being evaluated. (4)

The Croydon derailment and the subsequent mitigation efforts high-light the crux of ERM. The mitigation efforts are designed to reduce the probability of a derailment. For the most part, the mitigation – additional chevron signs, digital signage and in-cab alerts, are low cost. However, they come after a derailment which killed seven peo-ple and injured fifty more. The driver was determined to have been driving too fast. He was subsequently arrested. (4)

In 2017, TfL admitted fault for the accident. This means that victims and their families will not have to sue for compensation due the loss caused by the accident. In addition, TfL reduced the speed for all TfL light rails.

THE ERM QUESTION

The TfL Croydon accident Illustrates a fundamental ERM question which is: Is it worth it? This question is linked to questions citizens have asked and have answered after such a risk event. The questions are basic ones.

Further, in their minds, citizens already have the answers. The follow-ing are examples: Is derailment a common problem for trains? Their answer is: 'Yes'. Since derailments do occur, is it a significant risk when they do occur? Their answer is 'Yes'. Is it a risk, which can be mitigated to a degree? Their answer is 'Yes'.

Citizens want to know: Why was this risk, which has serious conse-quences, not dealt with before lives were lost?

For management the questions are: Could the lives of those five peo-ple have been saved? Could the reparations costs have been avoided in part or whole?

Helping management identify potential risks and take mitigative steps

PRACTICAL TIPS: MONITORING AND REVIEW

- System to identify and assess issues that may influence a risk should be developed.
- Risk mitigation efforts are reassessed to ensure they are working as intended.
- New treatments should be considered, if treatments are not effective.
- There is continual feedback on the quality of risk reporting and adjust as needed.
- Cost benefit analysis on controls should be conducted regularly.
- Risks can be dropped from the risk register based on change in total score.
- There should be a link to continuous improvement and auditing systems for sustained monitoring and improvement.
- Aspects of the risk management process, including the framework, are reviewed at least once a year.
- Risks and treatment are reviewed regularly.
- Provision for alerting the appropriate level of management review should be established based on the identification of new risks or changes to mitigative actions.
- Reporting is an integral part of the organization's governance and should enhance communications between citizens and the governing body.

to reduce any adverse impact is the purpose of ERM. Monitoring and reviewing helps ensure that adjustments to mitigative actions are made as needed, new risks are identified, and mitigative actions are taken early.

ERM CHALLENGES

- Failure to thoroughly document the ERM process.
- Failure to develop and maintain a regular risk management reporting schedule.
- Failure to make clear assignment of risk monitoring and reporting responsibilities
- Failure to review the effectiveness of the risk controls (mitigative efforts).
- Failure to act when new risks appear, or existing risk mitigation needs to be adjusted.

The practical tips provide the basic elements to be considered with respect to the monitoring and reporting on the ERM process.

SUMMARY

Monitoring and Review is a necessary and important step in the ERM process. It ensures that the risk identification and assessment process is continually examined and improved as necessary. It ensures that the governing body, management, employees and citizens are regularly apprised of the mitigation efforts. By continually reviewing existing risks, determining emerging risk and adding or modifying treatment, the organization ensures that resources are continually allocated in an effective manner.

KEY POINTS

- Risk reporting policy should be established.

- Management should monitor and maintain the reporting schedule.

- When new risks are identified management should act quickly to score them and establish mitigative actions.

- Once mitigative actions have been established, management should make sure someone has been assigned to monitor them.

- When treatment actions are not successful, management should reassess and adjust the mitigative actions.

CHAPTER 13:
COMMUNCATION AND
CONSULTATION

INTRODUCTION

The purpose of Communication and Consultation is to assist relevant stakeholders in understanding risk, the basis on which decisions are made and the reasons why particular actions are required. Communication seeks to promote awareness and understanding of risk and how to deal with it. Whereas, Consultation involves obtaining feed-back and information to support decision-making. Close coordination between the two should facilitate factual, timely, relevant, accurate exchanges of information.

PURPOSE OF COMMUNICATION AND CONSULTATION

Communication and Consultation should be continual throughout each step in the ERM process. ISO 31000:2018 indicates the goal is to:

- Bring different areas of expertise together for each step of the risk management process.

- Ensure that different views are appropriately considered when defining risk criteria and evaluating risks.

- Provide information to facilitate risk oversight and decision-making.

- Build a sense of inclusiveness and ownership among those affected by risk.

It should be recognized that the process links into existing communications activity. The author, for instance, wrote a weekly radio script on city activities for the Assistant City Manager. At various times the author made presentations before citizen groups, planning commissions, city councils, county commissioners and legislative subcommittees on programs, activities and laws. If one is a public sector manager and understands the process of communicating with staff, oversite bodies and the public, this step would be second nature. Communicating to various stakeholders' groups is part of the job.

In the ERM implementation stage, it is particularly important to communicate what ERM is and its value proposition. For ERM to be fully integrated into the daily work routine, a sense of ownership and participation needs to be felt and continually communicated. At one time or another, the identified risks, their scores and the treatment of those risks will have to be communicated to the governing body and employees throughout the various departments and work groups. The continual flow of information about risks and treatment options, enhances the viability and monitoring of the ERM process.

At the early steps in the ERM process, the risk management team and upper level management are the main stakeholders groups which require information. Once the risk evaluation step has been reached, the number of people that information needs to be obtained from and communicated with expands considerably.

PRACTICAL TIPS: COMMUNICATE AND CONSULT

- Determine who are the critical risk stakeholders and determine their information requirements.

- Communications approach should be documented.
- Stakeholder communication plan if relevant.
- Identify expertise required to provide advice about a risk.
- Communicate the importance of ERM regularly to the governing body, employees and the public.
- Regularly report the results of the risk mitigation efforts via the risk register to the governing body, employees and the public.

Up to the Monitoring and Review step, the communication process can be based on the decisions of upper level management and the risk management team leader. Once the Monitoring and Review step has been entered, a formal policy about what is transmitted and when, needs to be stated. In addition, the communication requirement should specify who is going to do the reporting.

COMMUNICATION GUIDE

The State of Victoria Australia has put forward a guide ensuring risk communications are effective. The guide is also a useful review for public sector communications in general. The goals are self-explanatory.

Risk communications will be most effective if guided by the following goals:

- **Plan for communications:** Communication efforts for decision makers and stakeholders need to be proactive as part of the risk management process. They should not be 'tacked on' at the end as an afterthought. Furthermore, risk information needs to be readily available for relevant parties at all stages of the risk management cycle.

- **Maintain trust:** Past communication efforts give context to the organization's next message, shaping how it will be received. Consistency is important, but only if it serves to build trust. When consistency is untenable considering emerging information, then officials need to acknowledge it, along with any errors that may be involved. This includes an explanation of what happened. Once trust is lost, it is very difficult to recover.

- **Use language appropriate to the audience:** When communicating risk, it is important to consider the intended audience and tailor the language and channels used to effectively convey the information to promote and elicit the desired actions and outcomes.

- **Be both clear and transparent:** Clarity and transparency are important to effective communications. Clarity means communicating in a direct, simple and understandable way. Transparency in communications means disclosing assumptions, methodology, and uncertainty are considered.

- **Respect the audience's concerns:** Risk communications are most effective when the recipient's concerns and/or issues are acknowledged. Maintaining open channels for collaboration or feedback fosters mutual understanding. Communicators should be both receptive and responsive to queries from decision makers and stakeholders.

ERM CHALLENGES

- Failure to be clear and transparent in communications.
- Failure to inform upper level management about new risks or risk whose impact is increasing.
- Failure to maintain integrity of the information.
- Failure to respect the audiences' concerns.

- **Maintain integrity of information**: Effective risk communications should acknowledge uncertainty, note any limitations of information, make assumptions explicit, and distinguish assertions from judgments supported by analysis and evidence. (1)

SUMMARY

Communication connects each step of the risk management process. It is also crucial for linking the risk management principles and process. One cannot overstate the importance of communications in risk management.

In order to effectively integrate ERM into the organization's culture and activities, the risks, their potential impact and the actions taken to alleviate or reduce these impacts need to be continually communicated.

KEY POINTS:

- It is important that communications should be continuous. Poor communications can lead to poor decision making. This, in turn, could jeopardize ERM's success.

CHAPTER 14:
ERM PERFORMANCE AUDITS

INTRODUCTION

In the previous chapters the need for and process of implementing ERM was presented. The benefits of implementing ERM have also been shown. This chapter shows the results of the ERM process. It discusses the results of two ERM performance audits.

The audits were designed to determine how effective the organizations, New South Wales and the Commonwealth of Australia have been in implementing ERM. These audits show the successes and deficiencies in implementing ERM. Consequently, they indicate that ERM can be successfully implemented at the state and national level. They also show that full integration is not a short-term process.

NEW SOUTH WALES AUDIT

NEW SOUTH WALES PERFORMANCE AUDIT

In 2012, the Treasury Department of New South Wales issued 'Risk Management Tool Kit for NSW Public Sector Agencies'. It was a guide to help implement the ERM mandate for NSW agencies. The guide is based on the International Organization for Standardization's 31000 (ISO 31000).

In 2018, the NSW Audit Office conducted an audit of four agencies to determine the extent of ERM implementation. The four agencies were Ministry of Health, NSW Fair Trading, NSW Police Force, and NSW Treasury Corporation.

The audit determined 65.5% of the employees said senior leaders are stressing the importance of ERM, and 80% of employees and managers believe ERM adds value. It also found that three of the four agencies had up-to-date frameworks for managing risk. These frameworks include:

- Risk appetite statement.

- Description of roles and responsibilities for managing risks.

- Description of the process for managing, monitoring, reporting and reviewing risks.

- Risk categories.

- Risk rating metrics.

PROBLEMS NOTED

Two of the problems noted in the audit report were: 1. Ensuring that employees feel comfortable communicating risk related problems to management. and 2. Ensuring that employees are recognized for managing and reporting risks. (1)

The audit indicates that ERM is well entrenched. Further, both management and employees indicate it adds value to the organization. Nevertheless, even after six years, additional work is needed to ensure ERM is fully integrated into agency operations.

AUSTRALIAN COMMONWEALTH PERFORMANCE AUDIT

In 2014, the Commonwealth of Australia adopted ERM. To facilitate implementation and follow up performance audits, it required all department and agencies to implement the twenty-two ERM related requirements. The requirements are linked to nine steps similar to ISO 31000:2018's steps.

A full listing of the steps, called elements and the requirements is provided in Appendix C. Below is an example from one of the steps. Responsibility for an entity's performance in managing risk lies with management.

DEFINE RESPONSIBILITY
Management must define the responsibility for managing risk by:

- "Defining who is responsible for determining an entity's risk appetite and tolerance for risk.

- Allocating responsibility for implementing the entity's risk management framework.

- Defining entity roles and responsibilities in managing individual risks." (2)

By including the elements and the requirements in the Risk Management Guide, Commonwealth management stated up front the expected performance requirements that departments and agencies were to carry out as they implemented ERM.

The listing of specific performance criteria also facilitates performance audits, because it provides the auditors with specific activities against which the ERM implementation progress can be measured.

In 2017, the Audit Office of the Commonwealth, conducted an ERM Compliance audit. (3) The objective of the audit was to determine the effectiveness of ERM implementation. Four agencies were audited. They were the Department of Employment (Employment), the Department of Health (Health), the Australian Communications and Media Authority (ACMA) and the Australian Fisheries Management Authority (AFMA). The criteria used to evaluate performance was the nine elements and twenty-two requirements.

AUDIT METHODOLOGY

Audits conducted by the Audit Office meet the same standards required of the auditing profession in Australia and are consistent with international public sector auditing standards. In undertaking the audit, auditors:

- Sought information from entity management on risk management performance.

- Reviewed relevant documents, including the risk management policies and frameworks of the four entities.

- Interviewed staff and reviewed relevant risk management records in a sample of business areas.

- Interviewed the chairs of entity audit committees.

- Examined information obtained by the Australian Public Service Commission (APSC) and from Comcover's annual self-assessment Risk Management Benchmarking Survey.

Agency	Met	Mostly met	Total	Percentage
Employment	19	2	21	95
Health	10	10	20	91
ACMA	6	10	16	73
AFMA	13	2	15	68

Table 21 - Audit Results

APSC conducts an annual survey of employees and agencies. Part of the survey deals with risk. The Department of Finance's insurance arm (Camcover) conducts an annual risk self-assessment which is used to benchmark agency performance.

AUDIT FINDINGS

Table 21 shows the overall audit results based on the twenty-two requirements for the four audited departments. The results indicate there is uneven application among the agencies. ERM is well entrenched in Employment and Health. ACMA and AFMA need additional work.

Looking at the individual agencies, the audit determined Employment has a well-integrated ERM framework for risk identification and management. It has implemented a range of measures to build its risk management capabilities. There is enterprise wide oversight through an internal governance committee. The committee reports regularly to the agency's Executive Committee on the adequacy of the risk management process.

Health has an ongoing program to strengthen and fully implement ERM. Key risks are regularly considered by the Health's Executive Committee in the development of strategic and operational plans.

ACMA's key risks are reviewed quarterly by senior management. ACMA has a risk tolerance statement in its risk management guide.

ACMA's risk management guide provides a high-level description of risk management. But it has limited guidance on how staff should manage risk.

The AFMA Commission looks at sustainability risks regularly when considering specific fisheries management strategies and plans.

AREAS OF IMPROVEMENT

Areas requiring improvement were:

- Defining the entity's risk appetite in their risk management policy.

- Improving the identification and management of shared risks.

- Developing arrangements for communicating, consulting and reporting on risk with internal and external stakeholders.

- Improving arrangements to regularly review risks, risk management frameworks and the application of risk management practices.

- Fully embedding the corporate plan requirement relating to risk.

- Assigning responsibility for risk management to individuals or positions, rather than work areas.

Commonwealth agencies have successfully implemented ERM. Employment and Health provide good models for other agencies and demonstrate that the Commonwealth is serious about ERM implementation. Nevertheless, work on ERM fundamentals is still needed.

COMCOVER SELF ASSESSMENT SURVEY

Since audits are only performed periodically, Comcover, the Commonwealth's self-insurance agency, conducts a self-assessment survey annually. The survey has two components. One is a survey of employees. The other is companywide.

EMPLOYEE SURVEY

The employee responses determined:

- Over 70% are aware of risk management policies and know where to find them.

- 59% said risks are managed proactively.

- Over 50% said "In my immediate work area employees respond to risk in a manner consistent with my entity's risk management policies and processes."

- Over 50% said "In general, my entity has effective risk management policies and procedures." (4)

The employee response indicates awareness of ERM policies. They believe the policies are being applied proactively. The high percentage in awareness indicate that management is communicating the importance of risk management to employees. Further, employees are taking risk management seriously and applying risk assessment in their workplace.

COMCOVER SELF ASSESSMENT SURVEY RESULTS

The Comcover Commonwealth wide benchmarking survey covered a total of 143 agencies. It is a self-assessment survey which examines six levels of risk maturity based on the nine ERM elements. The criteria defining each maturity is extensive.

Below are the six levels and a sampling of the criteria defining each.

1. Fundamental

    a. Risk management policy and framework endorsed by management.

    b. Risk appetite is consistently expressed.

2. Developed

    a. Risk management framework fully embedded in organization.

    b. Risk appetite statement is high level and qualitative.

3. Systematic

    a. Risk management framework supports a consistent approach to identification, assessment, evaluation and treatment.

    b. Risk profile enables the prioritization of audit and assurance activities.

4. Integrated

    a. Risk management policy and framework are embedded in operations and part of management framework.

    b. Risk appetite statement includes both qualitative and quantitative elements which are linked to business strategy.

5. Advanced

    a. Risk management policy is integrated with strategic and business plans and review and updated on a regular basis.

b. Risk appetite is articulated through a comprehensive set of risk appetite and tolerance statement including Key Performance Indicators associated with each risk.

6. Optimal

a. Risk management policy considers the management of risk as an integral part of the governance system, with clear links to the strategic and operational objectives.

b. The costs of risk activities are identified and managed within the operational budget. (5)

Table 22 shows the self-assessment ratings for the audited agencies.

The Employment and AFMA self-assessment are consistent with the audit results. Employment is 'Optimal' in the first five elements and advanced in the rest. It is ranked the highest. AFMA is lower in maturity than Health and ACMA. In the middle there are differences. The self-assessment gives ACMA better marks than the audit. For all 143 agencies, the self-assessment indicates:

- Most agency's risk management policies include the core components. (Element 1)

- Opportunities exist to expand risk identification techniques (Element 2).

- Key risk management roles and responsibilities are not often defined (Element 3).

Self-Assessment Rating

Risk Element	Employ-ment	Health	ACMA	AFMA
Risk Manage-ment Policy	Optimal	Advanced	Advanced	Systematic
Risk Manage-ment Framework	Optimal	Integrated	Advanced	Advanced
Defining Responsibil-ities	Optimal	Advanced	Integrated	Systematic
Embedding risk manage-ment	Optimal	Integrated	Advanced	Systematic
Developing positive risk culture	Optimal	Integrated	Advanced	Developed
Communi-cating Risk	Advanced	Systematic	Integrated	Systematic
Under-standing shared risk	Advanced	Developed	Advanced	Fundament
Managing risk capabilities	Advanced	Developed	Advanced	Integrated
Reviewing and improving	Advanced	Integrated	Integrated	Systematic

Table 22 Self-Assessment Results

- Few entities have regular processes for assessing risk culture (Element 5).

- Limited communication of risk information to external parties (Element 6 and 8).

- Highest proportion of entities scored a maturity of *Fundamental* (Element 7).

- Insufficient training is provided to some key risk management groups (Element 8).

- Opportunities exist for measuring, assessing and reporting risk management performance (Element 9).

The Camcover survey shows that every element needs additional work if ERM is to be embedded into the organizational culture. Training needs to be improved. More effort on measuring and assessing risks is needed. Risk reporting and communications also needs improvement.

SUMMARY

New South Wales and the Commonwealth of Australia have demonstrated through their performance audits the ability of organizations to implement ERM and integrate it into the organization's culture.

The Commonwealth listed specific actions that one takes as departments and agencies implemented ERM. The requirements are consistent with ISO 31000 standards. The requirements tell agencies what is expected and provides specific objectives auditors can examine.

While the audits show substantial integration and level of ERM sophistication, they also found that agencies have a way to go for full integration.

In addition, to the risk performance audit, the Commonwealth of Australia used two other means to assess the implementation of ERM. These are a survey of employees and a self-assessment completed by department and agency management. The survey shows that employees understand ERM and feel it makes a difference. The annual self-assessment survey tracks with the audit results. This indicates that self-assessment surveys can be useful in providing management with information that can help identify areas which need addition emphasis and support.

Overall, the audits show that ERM can be implemented and integrated into an organization's culture. This process can be facilitated by specifying performance requirements upfront. Surveys indicate that employees feel ERM is beneficial to organizational performance. Finally, annual self-assessments can assist management in identifying aspect of the ERM process which need to be strengthened and stresses.

KEY POINTS:

- It takes time for ERM to be fully implemented.

- ERM Implementation works.

- Employees see value in ERM.

- NSW and the Commonwealth of Australia have been effective in integrating ERM into the organizational culture.

CHAPTER 15:
CONCLUDING THOUGHTS

Enterprise Risk Management is fast becoming an organizational standard and minimum competency for public sector organizations and managers. Its adoption reflects the increased awareness of the risks that governments face, their increasing costs and the VUCA environment.

In addition to the ERM examples contained herein, other governments which have implemented ERM are listed in Appendix C. The number of adoptees provide multiple examples governments can draw upon. The examples also show the level of sophistication being achieved by adoptees at all levels of government.

RISK STANDARDS

There are two international ERM models which provide the basis for the ERM process. These are ISO 31000:2018 and COSO ERM. Both provide a standardized and objective based methodology, which can be used to implement a risk identification and treatment approach at the strategic, operational and project level.

However, ISO 31000 is more frequently cited as the ERM model in government. It is used in Australia, Canada, New Zealand, and the United Kingdom. In the U.S. it is the basis of the Federal Highway

Administration's ERM mandate to state departments of transportation. It is also the basis for Yuma County Arizona's ERM process.

U.S. federal agencies have been implementing ERM since 2015. As they become more comfortable with ERM, the processes outline in the Playbook will filter into their rules and guides.

The Playbook has already influenced the administrative structure recommended for use by the FHWA. The FHWA suggests an administrative structure like that included in the Playbook. It also lists specific skill sets to be included in the risk identification team.

In addition, NIST and FEMA have included ERM in their guides. NIST has designed its cybersecurity standards to be incorporated into the organization's ERM process. FEMA and other federal agencies, as exemplified in the draft Risk Mitigation Strategy, are seeking to develop a consistent risk management vocabulary and common risk management practices to be used by state, local and tribal governments. It is also likely the Playbook will influence their approach.

In Canada and the United Kingdom, the national level push to have state and local governments adopt ERM has been aided by efforts from both individual professionals and professional societies. In Canada, Internal Auditors regularly included ERM in audit recommendations to management and the governing body. In the United Kingdom, CIPFA and SOLACE worked to develop a Good Governance Framework which includes ERM. This framework has become a reporting requirement. Local Governments must analyze the risk they face and present their mitigative actions. The framework has also been adopted by the IFAC. The framework is to be used by accountants worldwide. The ERM steps included in the IFAC framework are consistent with ISO 31000:2018.

ISO 31000:2018 contains eight steps. These includes determination of scope and context, risk identification, risk analysis and risk evaluation. ISO 31000:2018 emphasizes the involvement of the governing body and management. If they are not committed to and involved in the ERM process, ERM will not be successful. Further, to ensure it effectiveness, ERM must be integrated into the daily activities of the organization. This includes the strategic and operation plans, budget and performance measures.

That this integration can be achieved is seen by the results of the New South Wales and Commonwealth of Australia ERM implementation audits. Both have departments which have been very successful in implementing ERM. The audits also indicate that it takes time for ERM implementation to be successful. Even after six years, in the case of New South Wales, some departments and agencies were lagging their contemporaries.

Increasingly, ERM's ability to protect resources and save money is being recognized. The National Institute of Building Sciences study shows that risk mitigation efforts can save as much as six dollars for every one dollar spent. Public sector managers are also finding that ERM helps them make better decisions and improves operational effectiveness.

LIST OF TABLES

Table 1   City of Vadodura Smart City Mitigation

Table 2   Relationship of ERM Steps

Table 3   Risk Appetite for Worcester Shire Council

Table 4   Management Framework and Policy Work Plan

Table 5   SWOT Analysis Concept

Table 6   SWOT Marion County Housing Authority

Table 7   SWOT Mogale City Local Municipality

Table 8   Example 1

Table 9   Risk Categories Warwick Shire County
            Council UK

Table 10   Example 2

Table 11   Consequence Rating Vale of Glamorgan Council

Table 12   Likelihood rating Vale of Glamorgan Council

Table 13   Example 3

Table 14   Argyll Bute Risk Register

Table 15   Example 4

Table 16   Clare & Gilbert Valleys Council Risk Decision State-
            ment

Table 17   Risk Register City of Saskatoon

Table 18   Risk Register Flooding Pump Station #4

Table 19   City of Glasgow Scotland Risk Report & Monitor
            Requirement

Table 20   City of Oshawa Risk Control Measures

Table 21   Audit Results

Table 22   Self-Assessment Rating

LIST OF FIGURES

Figure 1   Risk Management Structure

Figure 2   ISO 31000:2018 ERM Process

Figure 3   Heat Map

Figure 4   Risk Register Flow

INDEX

A

administrative benefits, 29
adverse impact, 15, 32, 40, 66,
   68, 80, 84, 117, 124, 126,
   137, 143, 146, 154, 155,
   161, 163
appetite levels, 83
audits, 72, 202
Australia, 22, 48
Australian Commonwealth,
   201
avoiding the risk, 159, 160

B

Baldrige framework, 69
Baltimore – police
   department, 39
brainstorming, 127, 137
Broome county New York –
   office of emergency service,
   39

C

Calgary – increasing insurable
   losses, 21
California wildfires, 20
categories, 98, 120, 123, 124,
   130, 131, 134, 137, 138,
   139, 146, 200

Chattanooga, 31, 70, 117,
   161, 163, 227
check list, 54, 55, 162
Chief Risk Officer, 89
CIPFA, 51, 53
City of Atlanta Georgia –
   ransomware cyber-attack,
   24
City of Windsor Canada, 89
Committee Of Sponsoring
   oOrganizations, 59
Commonwealth of Australia,
   10, 47, 53, 199, 201, 209,
   210, 213, 242
communication, 6, 31, 44, 62,
   103, 157, 161, 163, 171,
   183, 193, 195, 197
communication guide, 195
Condoleezza Rice, 12
consequence, 3
consequences, 34, 103, 119,
   120, 126, 141, 142, 149,
   160, 161, 167, 174, 189
context, 79, 82, 104, 109, 111,
   114, 117, 119, 120, 121,
   122, 123, 124, 128, 130,
   131, 135, 137, 196, 213,
   244
context, 5, 72, 103, 109, 114,
   120, 121
contingency plan, 175
COSO, 60

COSO ERM, 8, 59, 61, 62, 64, 66, 67, 68, 74, 75, 87, 102, 172, 211
CRO, 89
Croydon, 188, 189
customized, 65
cyber-security, 38, 45, 50, 51

D

denbighshire united kingdom, 28
digital government, 35
disaster risk reduction 2015-2030, 11

E

Eagle Creek wildfire, 19
effective controls, 89
electric power board, 31
Enterprise Risk Management, 60
environmental, 145
environmental social and governance, 12
ERM, 5, 6, 7, 8, 11, 12, 13, 14, 27, 28, 29, 30, 32, 34, 40, 43, 45, 47, 48, 49, 51, 53, 54, 55, 56, 57, 59, 61, 62, 64, 65, 66, 67, 69, 70, 71, 72, 74, 75, 77, 78, 79, 80, 84, 85, 86, 90, 91, 92, 93, 94, 95, 96, 98, 99, 100, 101, 102, 103, 106, 107, 111, 120, 124, 125, 130, 135, 137, 139, 151, 153, 157, 158, 163, 167, 171, 172, 173, 175, 181, 183, 187, 189, 191, 193, 194, 197, 199, 200, 202, 203, 204, 205, 209, 210, 211, 213, 215, 216, 227, 229, 230, 231, 235, 238, 242
executive management, 59
existing controls, 141, 154
external risk, 136

F

FDOT, 135, 136, 149, 165, 167
Federal Highway Administration, 8, 92, 101, 136, 212
FEMA, 12, 15, 32, 45, 48, 49, 51, 56, 163, 167, 212, 229
FHWA, 8, 92, 93, 101, 102, 136
fire suppression, 20
Flint Michigan water contamination, 24
Flint Michigan water crisis, 24
flooding, 17, 127, 128, 178, 179, 215, 224
flooding in thailand, 17
framework, 51, 52, 53, 60, 61, 69, 70, 79, 82, 84, 85, 86, 87, 90, 91, 102, 168, 190, 201, 203, 206, 223, 229, 230, 238, 242, 243, 244, 245
fraud, 24, 59, 97

G

Glamorgan, 144, 145, 146, 150, 215, 232
governance, 59, 70

governance and culture, 61
governing body, 79, 240
government, 48
government accountability
    office, 28, 227
Greater Geraldron City
    Council, 85

H

heat map, 142, 143, 144, 146,
    149, 150, 151
housing authority, 110, 111,
    114, 115, 116, 117, 147,
    160, 169, 215
housing money, 115

I

information, 45, 50, 62, 66,
    87, 97, 118, 126, 132, 133
infrastructure, 26
internal risk, 136
ISO 31000, 1, 7, 52, 56, 59, 62,
    65, 66, 67, 74, 75, 77, 79,
    85, 87, 98, 101, 102, 103,
    105, 106, 117, 120, 123,
    124, 130, 131, 137, 141,
    153, 155, 168, 172, 173,
    193, 199, 209, 211, 213,
    216
L

lean initiatives, 71
likelihood, 44, 73, 141, 144,
    146, 149, 150, 162, 174,
    176, 178, 215
Lloyd's of london risk
    assessment – risk event, 23

local government, 7, 12, 17,
    25, 26, 32, 43, 48, 54, 55,
    104

M

Macomb County sewage leak -
    human error, 25
management, 5, 7, 12, 15, 27,
    28, 29, 32, 34, 45, 47, 49,
    55, 59, 60, 64, 65, 70, 72,
    73, 74, 77, 80, 85, 86, 87,
    89, 90, 91, 92, 94, 97, 98,
    99, 110, 129, 133, 135, 138,
    139, 151, 157, 162, 184,
    199, 201, 202, 208, 211,
    215, 216, 223, 226, 227,
    228, 229, 230, 231, 232,
    233, 234, 235, 236, 237,
    242
management governing
    council, 95
management strategies, 183
Mayor Bloomberg, 24
Mckay Council Australia, 27
measurement, 52, 90, 126,
    184
Minnesota – vehicle licensing
    software, 39
mitigate flood damage, 44
mitigative effect, 179
mitigative efforts, 43, 50, 68,
    83, 84, 103, 105, 106, 109,
    121, 122, 154, 174, 177,
    183, 186, 187, 191
monitoring, 28, 35, 36, 40, 67,
    74, 87, 91, 105, 126, 144,
    153, 162, 167, 170, 175,

177, 181, 184, 186, 190,
191, 194, 195, 200, 238
monitoring, 5, 53, 64, 103,
133, 183, 184, 191, 215

N

National Academies of
Sciences, 34
National Institute of Building
Science study, 32
National Institute of
Standards and Technology,
50
National Oceanographic and
Atmospheric Damage
Assessment, 20
natural disasters, 10, 12, 15,
16, 17, 20, 21, 22, 23, 27,
33, 43, 45, 56, 57, 68, 102,
129, 161
New Orleans - preventive
maintenance issues, 25
New York City, 24
New Zealand, 48
NIST, 45, 48, 50, 51, 56, 162,
212

O

OMB playbook, 9, 49, 99
operational risk, 131
opportunities and strengths,
121
Oregon Eagle Creek wildfire,
19
Oregon Public Employee
Retirement System – legacy
system, 25

Oshawa Canada, 70, 185, 186
Ottawa Canada tornado, 19

P

Paradise California camp fire,
18
performance, 6, 53, 60, 62,
64, 69, 89, 97, 136, 176,
207, 229, 230, 234
performance management,
118, 184
PERS, 26
Ohiladelphia – streets
department, 39
playbook, 87
potential risks, 122, 128
president trump, 15, 43, 49
prevention, 12, 16
prevention plan, 97, 175
principles, 3
project impact, 174
public administration, 9
public risks, 23, 27

Q

Quality + Engineering, 3
Queensland Australia flood,
22

R

report, 187
reporting, 5, 62, 92, 97, 103,
153, 173, 184, 190, 215
reporting systems, 89, 180,
238
reputation, 24, 131

residual risk, 175

resilience, 33, 34, 163, 223, 225, 227, 233

review, 62, 97

reviewing, 53, 183, 191, 208, 244

risk, 5, 7, 11, 23, 28, 44, 55, 60, 63, 64, 65, 66, 70, 71, 72, 73, 74, 77, 80, 82, 83, 85, 86, 89, 90, 91, 92, 94, 95, 97, 99, 103, 105, 106, 107, 117, 120, 123, 125, 131, 134, 135, 136, 138, 141, 142, 146, 147, 148, 149, 150, 153, 156, 157, 159, 160, 163, 165, 166, 168, 171, 173, 174, 175, 176, 177, 178, 179, 180, 184, 185, 187, 191, 195, 196, 199, 200, 201, 202, 206, 207, 208, 209, 215, 216, 223, 225, 226, 227, 229, 230, 231, 232, 233, 234, 235, 236, 237, 242, 243

risk analysis, 40, 93, 105, 141, 142, 146, 213

risk appetite, 62, 68, 69, 80, 81, 82, 83, 84, 87, 98, 99, 105, 120, 122, 137, 153, 155, 158, 171, 172, 187, 201, 204, 207, 242

risk assessment, 12, 56, 62, 63, 93, 96, 97, 142, 174, 205

risk avoidance, 68

risk category, 130, 135, 137, 173

risk category, 174

risk concerns, 60

risk controls, 168

risk description, 174

risk evaluation, 73, 119, 125, 154, 156, 194, 213

risk events, 12, 15, 23, 32, 60, 66, 68, 106

risk identification, 43, 89, 93, 98, 102, 103, 111, 114, 121, 123, 137, 138, 173, 191, 203, 207, 213

risk management, 3, 7, 16, 27, 29, 34, 37, 45, 49, 50, 52, 53, 55, 56, 64, 65, 66, 68, 69, 70, 71, 72, 73, 74, 77, 78, 79, 80, 81, 82, 84, 85, 86, 87, 89, 93, 95, 97, 98, 99, 100, 101, 102, 106, 107, 109, 111, 125, 130, 135, 138, 153, 157, 159, 163, 165, 172, 179, 181, 183, 185, 187, 190, 191, 193, 194, 196, 197, 201, 202, 203, 204, 205, 206, 207, 209, 212, 234, 238, 242, 243, 244, 245

risk management council, 87

risk management policy, 70

risk management strategy, 97, 231

risk mitigation, 10, 31, 33, 41, 43, 54, 79, 96, 122, 159, 165, 179, 186, 213

risk owner, 175

risk rank, 174

risk register, 70, 91, 105, 125, 129, 130, 138, 147, 153, 163, 173, 174, 175, 179, 181, 183, 186, 190

risk register, 97, 130, 173
risk register flow, 180
risk treatment, 103, 170
risk trigger, 174

S

Saskatoon, 175, 177, 215, 233
scope, 5, 74, 103, 109, 120,
    121
service project reviews, 71
sharing, 161
silo boundaries, 110
smart building, 35
smart citizens, 36
smart city, 35, 38, 43, 215,
    228
smart energy, 36
smart governance and
    education, 35
smart healthcare, 35
smart infrastructure, 36
smart mobility, 36
smart technology, 36
social impacts, 22
solace, 51, 53
source, 161
State of Victoria, 124, 168,
    195
strategy and objective-setting,
    61
structured and
    comprehensive, 65
SWOT, 113, 114, 115, 116,
    117, 119, 121, 122, 123,
    137, 215, 231

T

TAMP, 8, 135, 232
technology, 97
threats, 113, 121, 122
transport for london: case
    study (3), 187
treatment, 21, 62, 66, 73, 77,
    90, 91, 92, 102, 109, 110,
    120, 124, 125, 138, 144,
    153, 154, 157, 159, 160,
    164, 165, 168, 169, 171,
    172, 173, 174, 175, 177,
    181, 186, 190, 191, 194,
    206, 211

U

U.S. Congress, 28, 48, 57
U.S. Department of Veterans
    Affairs medical care system
    failure, 23
United Kingdom, 51
United States federal
    government, 28
upper level management, 157,
    171

V

value, 60, 61, 65, 66
Veterans Administration, 23
Veterans Health
    Administration, 23
Victoria practice guide, 9
Visakhapatnam District in
    India, 18
Volkswagen, 31
VUCA, 17, 74, 169, 211

W

Warwick Shire County, 131,
    134, 215, 232
WBCSD, 64
wildfire mitigation, 43
wildfires, 127, 224
Worcester Shire, 29, 30, 82,
    83, 215
Worcester Shire Council, 29

ENDNOTES

Preface

1.	2018, "Extreme Weather Cost Europe Nearly Half A Trillion euros So Far", Eurativ
https://www.eurativ.com?sectin/climate-environment/news/ex-treme-weather-cost-eurpose-nearly-half-a-trillion-so-far.
2.	United Nations, 2015, "Sendai Framework for Disaster Risk Reduction 2915-2030", page 10, https://www.unisdr.org/ccordi-nate/sendai-framework.
3.	Ibid, page 10.
4.	Rice, Condoleezza and Amy B. Zegart, 2018, "Political Risk: How Businesses and Organizations Can Anticipate Global Insecurity", Twelve, New York,
5.	COSO, 2018, "Enterprise Risk Management: Applying Enterprise Risk Management To environmental, Social and Governance-related Risks", October, page 2.
6.	Ibid page 9.
7.	Shapiro, Gary, 2019, "What To Stand Out From The Crowd? Cultivate Resilience", SmartcitiesDive, April 3, https://www.smartcitiesdive.com/news/want-to-stand-out-from-the-crowd-cultivate-resilience/551938/.

Chapter 1

1.	Organization for Economic Cooperation and Development,2014, "OECD Reviews of Risk Management Policies: Boosting Resilience through Innovative Risk Governance: Executive Summary", www.oecd.org/gov/risk/executive-summary.pdf, page 3.
2.	"Actuaries. Government renew mitigation calls", March 4,

2019, https://www.insurance news.com.au/regulatory-government/actuaries-local-government-renew-mitigation-calls.

3. Reinsurance News, 2019, "Anon puts insured cat losses at 490bn in 2018, economic costs at $2.25bn", January 22, https://www.reinsurancecene.ws/

4. Ibid

5. Setboonsarng, Chayut, 2011, "Economic Damage of Thailand's Flooding", CogitAsia, October 25, https://www.cogitasia.com/economic-damage-of-thailand-floods/

6. Visakhapatnam, India, "Smart Cities Challenge Report", www.smartcities challenge.org/assets/cities/viza-india/, page 3

7. Mandel, Klya, 2019, "Insurance Company Overwhelmed by cost of California wildfire, goes out of business", Dec 6, https://thinkprogress.org/cost-of/California-wildfire-has-causual-an-insurance-company-to-go-out-of-business-47af8295e30/

8. Wikipedia, "Eagle Creek Fire", https://em.wikipedia.org/wiki/Egale-Creek-Fire

9. Britneff, Bearice, 2019, "Ottawa Tornadoes cost Hydro One, Hydro Ottawa $15.7M, utilities estimate", January, 29, https://globalnews.ca/news/4902154/ottawa-tornadoes-damage-hydro-one-hydro-ottawa/

10. Mitchell, R., 2018, "2018 Wildfires Will Cost California Total Economic Losses of $400 Billion", CDN, November 22, https://coservativelynews.com/2018/11/2018-wildfires-will-cost-california-total-economic-losses-of-400-billion.

11. U.S. Global Change Research Program, 2018, "Fourth National Climate Assessment: Volume II", https://nca2018global.chanes.gov

12. Cullen, David, 2018, "Government Report Calls for 20-Year Fix of Interstate Highways", December 5, HDT Truckinginfo, https://www.truckinginfo.com/320772/government-repor-calls-for-

20year-fix.

13.   Congressional Budget Office, 2019, "Expected Costs of Damage From Hurricane Winds and Storm Related Flooding", April, www.cbo.gov/publication/55019.

14.   City of Calgary, 2018, "#ResilientYYC:Preliminary Resilience Assessment", Mach, www.calgary.ca/CS/Documents/ResilienceCalgary/Calgary-PRA:100RC-Executive-Review-2018-03-08pdf

15.   Anon's Reinsurance Solutions, 2019, Insurance Covered 490B of Natural Disaster Losses in 2018, Leaving 60% Protection Gap", Insurance Journal, January 22, htts://www.insurancejournal.com/news/international/2019/01/22/515420

16.   Slezak, Michael, 2016, 'Natural Disasters Costing Australia 50% More Than Estimated', The Guardian, March 1.https://www.theguardian.com/world.com/mar/02/natural-disaster-costing-australia-50-more-than-estimated.

17.   Lloyd's of London, 2018, "Lloyd's City Risk Index: Executive Summary", https://www.lloyds.com/cityriskindex/files/8771-city-executivesummary-aw.pdf.

18.   Wikipedia, w014, "Veterans Health Administration Scandal 2014",en.wikipedia.org/wiki/Veternans-Health-Administratin-Scandal.

19.   Berstein Lenny and Brady Dennis, 2016, "Six More Michigan Employees Charged With Misconduct In Flint Water Crisis", The Washington Post, July 29.

20.   Heires, G.N., 2014, "Three Sentenced for $100 million Fraud in Botched Automated Payroll Project in New York City, The New Crossroads, April 30, https://the new crossroads.org.

21.   Federal News Radio, 2018, "City of Atlanta Computer Network Hit by Ransomware Attack", March 22, federalnewradio.com/technology-news/2018/03/city-of-Atlanta-computer-network-hit-by-

ransomeware-attack.

22. Hall, Chris, 2019, "tsunami of Sewage from 'Human Error' caused Michigan sinkhole, $70Mmillion in Damage", USA Today, January 9, https://www.msn.com/en-us/news/tsunami-of-sewage-from-uman-error-caused-michigan-sinkhole-dollar- 70-million-in-damage-/er-BBS29ic?ocid=spartandhp.

23. Wright, Pam, 2017, "New Orleans Officials Scramble to Repair Drainage Pumps and Turbines as Harvey Looms", The Weather Channel, August 24, https://weather.com/storm/hurricane/news/newor-leans-harvey-drainage-pumps.

24. Sickinger, Ted, "PERS: Oregon's Public Pension Costs Will Go Up $885M New Year", The Oregonian/OregonLive, www.ore-gonlive.com/political/2016/07/pers-oregons-public-pension-cohtml.

25. Street, Chris, 2019, "Trump Disaster relief Cut-off May Cost California $10Biliion", American Thinker, January 11, https://www.americanthinker.com/blog/2019/01/trump-disaster-re-lief-cut-off-may-cost-california-10-billion-html.

26. Carlson, Jonathan, 2019, "State Needs to Spend $12 Billion on Sewage, Water Infrastructure Improvements", January 4, https://www.cbs46.com/news/state-needs-to-spend-billions-on-sewage-water-infrastucture-improvemets/article-dc70g174-1010-11e9-cefcof2396.00.html

27. 2016, "Canadian Infrastructure Report Card: Informing the Future Key Message", candianinfrastucture.ca/downloads/candian-in-frastructure-report-card-key-message-2016pdf.

28. MacKay Regional Council, 2018, "Enterprise Risk Management" Policy No 049, www.mackayqld.au/-data/assets/pdf-file/009/78849/043-Enterprise-Risk-Management-Policy-adopted-12-September-2018.pdf

29. Denbighshire County Council, 2016, "Managing Risk for Better

Service Delivery: A Guide to Risk Management", page 5, www.den
bighshire.gov.uk.

30.   United States Government Accountability Office, 2019, "High-
Risk Series: Substantial Efforts Needed to Achieve Greater Progress on
High-Risk   Areas"   ,   March,   GAO-10-157SP,   page   44,
https://www.gao.gov/products/gao-19-157sp.

31.   Office of Management and Budget, 2016, "Playbook: Enterprise Risk Management for the U.S. Federal Government", page 6,
https://cfo.gov/wp-content/uploads/2016/07/Final-ERM-Ply-
book.pdf.

32.   National Association of Counties, 2018, "Yuma County Earns
National Achievement Award for Enterprise Risk Management",
https://www.yumacountyaz.gov/Home/compo-
nents/jnews/new/2115/188.

33.   Worcester County Council, 2014, "Risk Management Policy
Statement and Strategy", page 3, worcesterhire.moderngov.docu-
ments/s3525/cab%2020141218%%20risk-background%20doc.pdf.

34.   Glass, Jim, Alex Melin, Benn Ollis and Michael Starke, 2015,
"Chattanooga Electric Power Board Case Study – Distribution Automation", ORNL Report Number: ORNL/LTR-2015/444, pp. 1-11.

35.   Op cite Lloyd's City Risk Index: Executive Summary

36.   National Institute of Building Sciences, 2017, "Natural Hazard
Mitigation Saves: 2017 Interim Report", https://www.fema.an/natu-
ral-hazard-mitigatin-saves-2017-interim.

37.   City of Calgary, 2018, "Climate Resilience Strategy: Mitigation
& Adaptation Action Plans'", page 6, www.calgary.ca/UEP/ESM/Doc-
uments/EMS-Documtnets/Climate -Resilience-Plan.pdf.

38.   Willis, Henry H. and Kathleen Loa, 2015, "Measuring the Resilience of Energy Distribution Systems:, Rand Corporation, page 3,

https://wwwenergy.gov/sites/prod/files/2015/07/134/QER%20Anal-lysis%30-%20Measuring%20the%20the%20Resilience%20of%20En-ergy%30Distribution%20System.pdf

39.   The Center for Infrastructure Protection & Homeland Security, 2017, The CIP Report", July 6,

40.   https://cip.gmu.edu/2017/07/06/resilience-risk-management-smart-cities.

41.   Ibid, page 2.

42.   Ibid page 2.

43.   Ibid page 2.

44.   Varghese, Romy, 2019, "America's Cities Are running on Software From the 80's", Bloomberg Business Week, February 28, page 1, https://www.bloomber.com/articles/2019-02-28/american's-cities-are-running-on-software-from-the-80's.

45.   ICMA, 2018, "Smart Communities: Rethinking Infrastructure", page 2, https://www.icma.org/document/smart-communities-re-thinking-infrastructure-report.

46.   Ibid page 3

47.   Alliance for Innovation, 2018, "Becoming a Flood-Resilient Region: StormSense meets Data Science", Case Study, September 1, 2017, https://www.transforminggov.org/case-

studies.

48.   City of Vadodara, 2016, "The Smart City Challenge Stage 2: Smart City Proposal", Smart City Code GJ-04VAD, pages 33-34, vado-darasmartcityin/vacdi/assets/report/proposal.pdf.

Chapter 2

1.   Federal Emergency Management Agency, 2018, "Draft National Mitigation investment Strategy, January 11, page1,

https://www..fema.gov/media-library-data/15568801146-ef9a295dc439odc0b032/Draft-National-Investment-Strategy-for-Public-Jan2018pdf.

2.   Federal Emergency Management Agency, 2018, "FEMA Disaster Recover Reform Act of 2018, https://www.fema.gov/disaster-recover-reform-act-2018.

3.   McGarth, Cheryl, 2019, "Risk Takes Centre Stage in 2019", ITWC Talks, January 21, https://www.itworldcanada.com/spansave/risk-take-centre-stage-in-2018.

4.   International Federation of Accountants,2014, 'International Framework: Good Governance In The Public Sector", July 2, page 27, https://www.ifac.org/publications-resources/international-framework-good-governance-public-sector.

5.   Effective Governance, Public Governance, performance and Accountability Act 2013, https://www.effectivegoverance.comau/public-governance-performance-accountability-act-2013-cthl.

6.   New South wales Local Government Agency, "Promoting Better Practices — Tools & Checklist", https://www.olg.nsw.gov.au/strengthening -local government/supporting-advising-councils/promoting/better/practice-review/program-tools-stretegic-framework-assessment-and-pracice-checklist.

Chapter 3

1.   COSO 2017, "Enterprise Risk Management Integrating with Strategy and Performance Executive Summary", June, page 1, https://www.coco.org/Documents/2017-COSO-ERM-Integrating_with_Strategy-and_Performance-Executive-Summary.pdf.

2.   COSO, 2016, "Public Exposure draft: Enterprise Risk Management: Integrating with Strategy and Performance: Executive

Summary", June, page 1, https://www.coso.org/Documents/COSO-ERM-draft-Post-Expenditures-versuib.pdf.

3.   COSO, 2017, opt cite, page 7.

4.   COSO 2016, opt cite. Page 62-63.

5.   International Organization for Standards, 2017, "ISO FDIS 31000:   Risk   Management   -Guidelines",   page   3, https://www.scric.com/articles/ISO-FDIS31000.pdf.

6.   Cohen, Michelle, 2017, "Study: New York City Could Get Hit With A Flood Every Five Years Instead of Every 500", 6SQFT, https://www.6sqft.com/study-new-york-city-could-get-hit-with-a-flood-every-five-years-instead-of-every-500.

7.   International Organization for Standardization, 2015, opt cite. Page 4.

8.   National Institute of Standards and Technology, 2017, Malcolm Baldrige Performance Excellence Framework 2017-2018", page 43,   https://www.nist.gov/baldrige-performance-excellence-framework.

9.   Ibid, page 50.

10.   City of Oshawa, 2017, Public Report: Corporate Risk Management Policy and Procedure", https://oshawa.ca,file C-100.

Chapter 4

1.   Northumberland County Council, 2016, "Risk Management Framework", July, page 3, www.northumberland.gov.uk.

2.   Ramotshere Moila Local Municipality, 2013, "Risk Management Policy Framework", Dec. page 7, www.ramotshere.gov.za/sites/default/files/documents/RML%20Risk%Magmt%20Policy%20Frame%20MAIN%20Doc-%20Find-D.pdf.

3.   Worcestershire County Council, 2014, "Risk Management

Policy Statement and Strategy", May, www.worcestershire.gov.uk, page 5.

4.   Ibid page 6.

5.   City of Geraldron City Council, 2015, "Risk Management Framework", April, page 3, https://www.cgg.wa.gov.au.

6.   Ibid page 3.

7.   City of Windsor, 2015, "Enterprise Risk (ERM) Framework'" April, page 15, https://www.City of Windsor.ca/cityhall/city-council-meetings-meetings-this-week/Documents/kAppendix%201%20En-terprise%20Risk%20Management%20Framework%20Risk%20-2015-04-08b%20To%20council.pdf.

8.   Ibid pages 18-19.

9.   Mohokare Local Municipality, 2012, "Risk Management Strat-egy, Framework & Policy, RMS002", July 16, Mohokare South Africa. page 3-4, www.mohokare.gov.za/document/strategies/revisedrisk-management

Chapter 5

1.   Federal High Way Administration, 2012, "Risk-Based Asset Management: Examining Risk-based Approaches to Transportation Asset Management Report 2 Managing Asset Risks At Multiple Levels In a Transportation Agency", Washington D.C. page 19.

Chapter 6

1.   Amadeo, Kimberly, 2018, "Hurricane Harvey Facts, Damage and Costs", The Balance, May 31, https://www.heblance.com/hurri-cane-harvey-facts-damage-cost-4150087/

2.   U.S. Office of Benefits Administration, 2016, Office of Benefits Administration/ERM-2016-Kronopolus-Leverging-SWOT.pdf

3.   Mogale City Local Municipality, 2009, "Revised Turn Around Strategy 2009-2014", www.mogalecity.gov.za/content/pdfs/strategic-planpdf.

4.   Victoria State Government, 2016, "Practice Guide", page 23, www.vmia.vic.gov.au/risk/risk-tools/risk/management/guide.

Chapter 7

1.   Victoria State Government, 2016, opt cite, page 28.

2.   Ibid page 24

3.   Ibid page 24

4.   Warwick Shire County Council, 2014, "Risk Management Framework", www.warwickshire.gov.uk/riskmanagementstrategy, page 13.

5.   Florida Department of Transportation, 2015, "Florida Transportation Asset Management Plan Technical Report", September 3, pages 3-3-3-4, www.floridadot.gov/planning/TAMP/technical report.pdf.

Chapter 8

1.   Vale of Glamorgan, 2018 "Risk Management Strategy 2018-2020, March, www.valeofglamorgan.gov.uk/documents.

2.   Argyll Bute, 2013, "Updated Strategic Risk Register Appendix A," https://www.argyll-bute.gov.uk/moderngov/documents/s82523

3.   Wychavon District Council, 2017, "Corporate Risk Register - 12th   May   2017",   https://www/wucjavpm/gpv/uk/docments/10586/8951431/Corporate+Risk+Registeer+July+2018.

4.   Florida Department of Transportation, opit cite, pages 3-4.

Chapter 9

1.   Clare & Gilbert Valley Council, 2016, "Risk Management Policy", June 20, page 15, https://claregilbertvalley.sa.gov.au/webdata/resources/files.

Chapter 10

1.   Organization for Economic and Community Development, 2014, "Boosting Resilience through Innovative Risk Governance: Executive Summary", www.oliverwyan.comcnttent/dam/oliver-wyman/global/on/2014/may/OECD%20-%20Boosting%20Exec%20Summary.

2.   Florida Department of Transportation, 2015, opit cite, pages 3-3-3-4.

Chapter 11

1.   Kloman, Vivian, 2018, "Key Elements of a Project Risk Register", continuingprofessionaldeveloent.org/key-elements-project-risk-register-template.

2.   City of Saskatoon, 2016, "Update on Key Strategic Risks", May 30, Saskatoon Canada, page 17. https: www.saskaton.ca.sites/default/file/document. Also see Corporate Risk 2017 Annual Report.

Chapter 12

1.   Glasgow City Council, 2009, "Risk Management Strategy", page   11,   https://www.glasgow.gov.uk/CHHpHandlerashX?d=7929&p=0.

2.   City of Oshawa, 2017, "Corporate Risk Management Policy and Procedures, Report Number CM-17-27" September 21, page 813,

app Oshaw.ca/agendas/City-Council/2017/09-2502017/Report-Cm-1727pdf.

3.　　　　Transportation for London, 2015, "Strategic Risk Management update – Quarter 1 2015", content.tfl.gov.uk/aac-20151008-part-1-item15-strategic-risk.

4.　　　　Wikipedia, "2016 Croydon tram derailment", https://emwikipedia.org/wiki/2016, -croydon-tram-derailment.

Chapter 13

1.　　　　Victoria State Government, 2016, "Practice Guide", page 28, www.vmia.vic.gov.au/risk/risk-tools/risk management guide.

Chapter 14

1.　　　　Audit Office New South Wales, 2018, "Managing Risks in the NSW Public Sector: risk culture, and capability", April 23, https://www.audit.nsw.gov.au/our-work/reports/managing-risks-in-the-NSW-public-sector-risk-culture-capability.

2.　　　　Australian Government Department of Finance, 2014, "Commonwealth Risk Management Policy", July 1, https://www.finance.gov.au/commonwealth-risk-managment-policy.pdf

3.　　　　The Auditor General, 2018, "he Management of Risk by Public Sector Entities" ANAO Report No 6 2017-18 Performance Audit, page 29, www.anao.gov.au>work>Performance Audit.

4.　　　　Ibid page 23.

5.　　　　Australian Government Department of Finance, 2017, "Benchmarking Marking Survey 2017 – Risk Management Capability Maturity Model", www.finance.gov.au/sites/default/files/risk-managment-capability-maturity-level.pdf.

Other Examples:

Risk Management Policies and Guides

Office of Risk Management Washington State, "Risk Management Basics", 2017

Western Australian, "Government Risk Management Guidelines", Sept 2014

British Columbia, "Enterprise Risk Management (ERM) Guidelines, 2006

Hobart City Council, "Risk and Audit Panel", 2015

Central Desert Regional Council, "Risk

Management Policy and Framework", 2014

Noosa Council, "Council Policy Risk Management", 2014

City of Perth, "Audit and Risk Committee Report", 2014

Toowoomba Regional Council, "Enterprise Risk Management", 2018

City of Edmonton, "Enterprise Risk Management", 2016.

City of Red Deer, "Integrated Risk Management Framework, 2017

City of Toronto, "Implementing an Integrated City-wide Risk Management Framework" 2015

Mbombela Local Municipality, Risk Management Policy, 2013.

Leeds City Council, "Corporate Risk Report", 2016

Bolton Council, "Risk Management Policy Statement", 2013

Bradford Borough Council, "Risk Management Strategy", 2016.

California State Leadership Accountability Act Biannual Risk Assessment Reports – selected departments

Department of Community Services and Development, Dec 30, 2015

Energy Resources Conservation and Development Commission, Feb 26, 2016

Business, Consumer Services and Housing, Dec 29, 2017

Department of California Highway Patrol, Dec 21, 2017

Department of Forestry and Fire Protection, Jan 02, 2018

The examples show the risk that are reported by a variety of California state agencies.

State Department of Transportation early adopters

Colorado Department of Transportation, "CDOT's Risk-Based Asset Management Plan", Dec 9, 2013.

Louisiana Department of Transportation, "Initial Transportation Asset Management Plan (Pilot Version Feb 2015)

Risk Registers

Table Land Regional Council, Corporate Risk Register, 2015

Manningham Council Six Monthly Strategic Risk Register Report, June 20, 2018

Powys County Council, "Corporate Risk Register, 2018.

Dacorum Borough Council, "Strategic Risk Register, 2017

Gloucester City Council Strategic Risk Register, 2017

Yorke Peninsula Council Strategic Risk Register 2016-20.

Merthyr Tydfil County Borough, "Annual Risk Management Progress and Update Corporate Risk Register, 2013-14.

Risk Implementation Assessment

Oulasvirta, Lasse and Ari-Veikko Anttiroiko, 2017, "Adoption of Comprehensive Risk Management in Local Government", Local Government Studies, Issue 43, Vol 3, pages 451-474

Meyer, N, 2014, A critical Analysis of Risk Management Knowledge within the Sedibeng District Municipality, South Africa", Mediterranean Journal of Social Science, Vol 3, No 7, May 2014, pages 163-170.

Canada Border Service Agency, 2014, "Audit of Enterprise Risk Management" December

APPENDIX A

Question Developed by Queensland Treasure Australia to Assist with ERM Implementation

Questions	Yes	No
• Has executive management or governing body developed and implemented a robust risk management framework appropriate for the size of the organization?		
• Does the organization have the necessary policies and procedures in place to support risk management?		
• Does the organization ensure all staff are aware of the risk management framework?		
• Does the organization have an explicitly state risk management policy that complements the organization's vision and strategic objectives?		
• Is there a designated risk management champion for the organization and operating units to oversee the implementation of an integrated risk management process?		
• Does risk management have the demonstrated support and ongoing attention of executive management?		
• Does the organization have a risk management committee which is responsible for overseeing the implementation of an integrated risk management process?		
• Is risk management communicated, understood and applied throughout the organization?		
• Is risk management integrated into existing		

governance and decision-making structures and performance reporting systems?		
• Have control and accountability systems been adapted to account for risk management processes?		
• Have key risk performance indicators and critical success factors been identified and included in organizational reports?		
• Does reporting on risk and risk management take place through existing management processes (e.g. performance reporting, ongoing monitoring, appraisals, internal auditing)?		
• Has the organization put in place effective initiatives to build risk management awareness?		
• Is written guidance (framework, policy or operating principles) communicated throughout the agency to support the integration of risk management principles into the daily operations of operational units?		
• Is risk management integrated into strategic and operational planning?		

APPENDIX B

Questions used by governing body and executive Management to make risk mitigation decisions

1. What is the cost of taking action in the short and long term?

2. What is the cost of not taking action in the short and long term?

3. Does the city have the available funds?

4. Does the city have staff and technical capacity to
   a. implement the decisions?

5. How will the decision align with the city's sustainability goals?

6. WIll the decision impact/affect regulatory requirements?

7. How do regulatory requirements impact/affect the
   a. decision?

8. What are the legal ramifications that should be
   a. considered?

9. What is the impact/effect on the city's reputation?

10. What will the effect be on other municipalities/cities?

11. How does the decision align with the city's strategic
    a. objectives?

12. How does the decision align with the city's operational objectives?

APPENDIX C

Commonwealth of Australia ERM Requirements

Element One: Establishing a Risk Management Policy.

A.   An entity must establish and maintain an entity specific risk management policy that:

- Defines the entity's approach to the management of risk and how this approach supports its strategic plans and objectives.
- Defines the entity's risk appetite and risk tolerance.
- Contains an outline of key accountabilities and responsibilities for managing and implementing the entity's risk management framework.
- Is endorsed by the entity's accountability authority.

Element Two: Establishing a Risk Management Framework.

A.   An entity must establish a risk management framework which includes:

- The overarching risk management policy (Element One)
- An overview of the entity's approach to managing risks.
- How the entity will report risk to both internal and external stakeholders.
- The attributes of the risk management culture that the entity seeks to develop, and the mechanisms employed to encourage it.
- How the entity contributes to managing any shared or cross jurisdictional risks.
- How the risk management framework and entity risk profile will be periodically reviewed and improved.
- The risk management framework must be endorsed by management.

Element Three: Defining responsibility for managing risk.

A. Within the risk management policy, the accountable authority of the entity must define the responsibility for managing risk by:

- Defining who is responsible for determining an entity's appetite and tolerance for risk.
- Allocating responsibility for implementing the entity's risk management framework.
- Defining entity roles and responsibilities in managing individual risks.

Element Four: The objective of effective management is to improve organizational performance. Considering risk is an integral element of the overall management capability of an entity and must include, and not be limited to, each of the following: strategic planning; the establishment of governance arrangements; policy development; program delivery; and decision making.

A. Each entity must ensure that the systematic management of risk is embedded in key business processes.

Element Five: Developing a positive risk culture.

A. Risk culture is the set of shared attitudes, values and behaviours that characterize how an entity considers risk in its day-to-day activities.

B. A positive risk culture promotes an open and proactive approach to managing risk that considers both threat and opportunity. A positive risk culture is one where risk Is appropriately identified, assessed, communicated and managed across all levels of the entity. Such a culture needs to be fostered and practiced by each entity.

C. An entity's risk management framework must support the development of a positive risk culture.

Element Six: Communicating and consulting about risk.

A. Communicating and consulting about risk underpins the success-ful management of risk. Effective communication requires con-sultation with relevant stakeholders and the transparent, com-plete and timely flow of information between decision makers.

B. Each entity must implement arrangements to communicate and consult about risk in a timely and effective manner to both inter-nal and external stakeholders.

Element Seven: Understanding and managing shared risk.

A. Shared risks are those risks extending beyond a single entity which require shared oversight and management. Accountability and responsibility for the management of shared risks must include any risks that extend across entities and may involve other sec-tors, community, industry or other jurisdictions.

B. Each entity must implement arrangements to understand and contribute to the management of shared risks.

Element Eight: Maintaining risk management capability.

A. Effective risk management requires an entity to maintain an ap-propriate level of capability to manage its own risk management program and to manage its risks. The nature and state of this ca-pability must be considered in the context of the entity's current resource and capability profile and be commensurate with the characteristics and complexity of its risk profile.

B. Each entity must maintain an appropriate level of capability to both implement the entity's risk management framework and manage its risks.

Element Nine: Reviewing and continuously improving the manage-ment of risk.

A. Formalizing and implementing risk management within an entity is not a "one-off-event". The effective management of risk is a process of continuous improvement, requiring regular review and evaluation mechanisms.

B. Each entity must review its risks, its risk management framework and the application of its risk management practices on a regular basis, and implement improvements arising out of such reviews.

www.ingramcontent.com/pod-product-compliance
Lightning Source LLC
Chambersburg PA
CBHW030501210326
41597CB00013B/753